"I very much enjoyed **The Spousal Equivalent Handbook.** It answered my questions in an easy to read format. I appreciated the quotes at the beginning of the chapters. And I liked the humor."

A SPOUSAL EQUIVALENT FROM SAN ANTONIO

"This readable handbook is up to date and highly recommended..."

LIBRARY JOURNAL

"(A) brightly written book..."

ALBANY TIMES–UNION

"Tips for two who live together."

THE HOUSTON CHRONICLE

"...covers virtually every legal and financial question on the subject."

ANCHORAGE TIMES

"Significant facts for significant others..."

HOUSTON TRIBUNE

Ten Commandments
for Spousal Equivalents

1. Realize that you and your partner have no legal relationship--this is the good news and the bad news. You have the flexibility to define your own rights and obligations, but if they are not in writing the rest of the world won't know what they are.

2. Find out about the laws in your state that affect unmarried couples. For example, it is against the law in several states for an unmarried man and woman to live together.

3. Determine whether or not your state still recognizes common-law marriage, and if your relationship has created one of these "informal" marriages.

4. Find out your state's view on "palimony" and whether or not the courts will honor contracts between spousal equivalents.

5. Verbalize your agreement on sharing expenses and acquiring property with your partner. Discover areas where you agree and areas that require compromise.

6. Consider drawing up a cohabitation agreement. It serves a three-prong purpose because it covers yesterday, today and tomorrow's property and money issues, and has the same effect as a pre-marital agreement if a couple marries.

7. Maintain separate finances, including bank accounts, savings and investments, to simplify record-keeping and tax filing.

8. Have a valid will prepared. Estate planning and financial planning are particularly important for spousal equivalents because they have no inheritance rights, nor do they share in each other's pension plans.

9. Discuss preparing a medical power of attorney to allow your partner hospital visitation and the right to make medical decisions in the event of an emergency.

10. Find out if your company, or any organization to which you belong, makes special arrangements for spousal equivalents. If not, question the policy.

THE
SPOUSAL
EQUIVALENT
HANDBOOK

THE
SPOUSAL
EQUIVALENT
HANDBOOK

by

Johnette Duff, J. D.
and
George G. Truitt, C.P.A., C.F.P.

SUNNY BEACH PUBLICATIONS   HOUSTON

Coming Soon from Sunny Beach Publications:

For Better or For Worse? A legal and financial guide to marriage *by Johnette Duff, Attorney at Law, and George G. Truitt, C. P. A. and Certified Financial Planner.* (Fall 1991)

Divorce: A legal and financial guide for women. *by Johnette Duff, Attorney at Law, and George G. Truitt, C. P. A. and Certified Financial Planner.* (Spring 1992)

Divorce: A legal and financial guide for men. *by Johnette Duff and George G. Truitt, C. P. A. and Certified Financial Planner.* (Spring 1992)

Tax Tips for Authors and Artists *by George G. Truitt, C. P. A. and Certified Financial Planner.* (Fall 1991)

Dedicated to my
spousal equivalent
and to you and yours.

For information, address Sunny Beach Publications, 2180 N. Loop W., Suite 120, Houston, Texas 77018.

Book Design by Nonnie
Cover Design by Amy Bass-Wilson

Duff, Johnette and George Truitt
    The Spousal Equivalent Handbook
        A legal and financial guide to living together.

ISBN 0-9627760-0-9
Library of Congress Catalog Card Number 90-71485
Printed in the United States of America

10 9 8 7 6 5 4 3 2

        Publisher's Cataloging in Publication
            (Prepared by Quality Books Inc.)
Duff, Johnette, 1951-
    The spousal equivalent handbook: a legal & financial guide to living together / Johnette Duff and George G. Truitt. --
        p. cm.
    Includes index
    ISBN 0-9627760-0-9

    1. Unmarried couples -- legal status, laws, etc. -- United States--Popular works. I. Truitt, George G., 1945- II. Title.

    KF538.Z9   346.73016
                              90-71485

Contents

ACKNOWLEDGMENTS

The inspiration for this book started with a car accident, when a young man made the unfortunate mistake of running a red light on a Friday the 13th and hitting and injuring a lawyer in another car. After spending too much time at the doctor and none at all at the health club, the lawyer decided that a leave of absence on her gym membership would save $90.00 a month and help pay the doctor bills.

While explaining to the membership director that she hoped to be back in action soon, based on the fact that she had actually managed to prepare two or three evening meals the week before, the membership director asked the fateful question.

"Do you and George live together?"

She knew we weren't married and no woman in her right mind and in physical pain would cook dinner just for herself. Plus, she lives with her "boyfriend."

That's when she explained that Johnette didn't need her own membership at the health club. She could be added for no additional charge under the family plan on George's membership if we would sign a document which stated that we lived together as domestic partners. Since Texas recognizes informal marriages, the director told us that several men, including some attorneys, had been reluctant to sign on the dotted line. After reading the document, which stated that the parties were *not* married, it was obvious it could actually be used to disprove a "common-law" marriage, as well as save $90.00 a month.

And that started the wheels turning. How many other organizations were beginning to recognize that living together is no longer just an alternative lifestyle? Was George entitled to any compensation due to the inconveniences he suffered when a third party ran a red light and injured his partner? And what about our commingled assets? What if something happened to one of us? What if we broke up?

We began our research with our own questions, and found many others. It became obvious that a lot of people could benefit from the answers.

If we haven't answered one of yours, let us know. Photocopy the form on the last page, fill it out and drop it in the mail. We'll try to incorporate new information in future editions of this book.

We would like to thank Debbie Pepper for getting the ball rolling, Mike Russell for his efforts to hold things together, and Dwight Espensen for his continued interest in the computer and its typefaces. Also thanks to Sandy Sheehy, Gary Bonnert, Jani Deters, Ken Fontenot, Gregg and Margaret Russell, Katherine Sandberg, Mary Steck, Sharon MacLean, and Lisette Wenck for reading our manuscript in progress and/or making invaluable suggestions.

Johnette Duff and George Truitt
Houston, Texas

INTRODUCTION

I was married once, but now I just lease.

from the movie *Buddy, Buddy*

Few developments relating to family life have been as dramatic as the increase in the number of unmarried couples living together in our country today. As conventional marriage proves less and less capable of delivering on its potential, living together can no longer be dismissed as merely an alternative lifestyle.

This book is a legal and financial guide to domestic unions outside matrimony. "Living together" is subject to many different interpretations, but for our purposes, the term will refer to a situation where two people (either opposite sex or same sex) cohabit, have a sexual relationship, and experience economic and social integration, i.e. where two people have created their own definition of "family." The moral implications of living together are outside the scope of our discussion and will not be mentioned except as they affect the law.

Living together offers an opportunity to define your own terms in a relationship, terms which are different from the traditional contractual rights and duties in a marriage. Even if the absence of a license is not a matter of choice, as in the case of same sex couples denied the option of becoming actual spouses, this flexibility is a major advantage of cohabitation.

Another attraction of living together has been the perception that the financial consequences of property division on divorce could be avoided, as well as the potentially costly legal procedures needed to end a marriage. But attempting to avoid the problems inherent in a marriage by avoiding the license is no guarantee.

Forming a partnership of any kind has inherent problems during formation and, certainly, upon dissolution. Living together is a partnership which has a lot of the same ups and downs as marriage. A little knowledge and careful planning is needed for the protection of both parties.

What is a spousal equivalent?

Serious issues aside for the moment, it's time to find a socially and legally accepted term that unequivocally describes unmarried domestic partners.

Are you bracketed together as a couple so often that you start feeling like there's an ampersand between your names, like bacon & eggs, Farrah & Ryan, or hot & cold? Do you stumble over introducing yourself as her "boyfriend" even more than you would over the "H" word? What if you're more than a girlfriend, but not ready to be a wife?

"Significant other" may have been a fine phrase for the 80's, but the 90's are here and it's time for a new term.

Lover may be an apt appellation, but try using it without blushing. Roommate may describe one aspect of your relationship, but doesn't come close to summing up the whole. The word homemate falls into the same category.

Legalese uses nonmarital or quasi-marital partners. Cohabit can be twisted into a noun such as cohabitor, cohabitant, cohabitator, but twists your tongue at the same time. One writer for Newsweek suggested the novel term "s'pose", as in "Do you s'pose they'll ever get married?"

The term consort has been suggested, but invokes visions of royalty. So does concubine, defined as a woman living with a man outside of legal wedlock.

There's also old lady and old man, but that creates the problem of whether or not someone is referring to their parent. The use of these terms will also tend to date you—although we all may have fond memories of the 60's, it's time to leave that language behind.

Mothers who have had to cope with a child setting up housekeeping in lieu of walking down the aisle have come up with the novel terms "sin-in-law" or "daughter-out-law."

"Spousal Equivalent" gets our nomination as the term that comes closest to describing a domestic partner. It succinctly sums up the situation, placing you firmly in that large gray area between "just friends" and "husband and wife."

If you feel you qualify for spousal equivalent status, keep reading and we'll help you step through the minefields that face those who have earned the title.

Know your rights as a Spousal Equivalent

In the following chapters, we will cover the concept of informal, "common-law" marriage, and the more nebulous concept of "palimony." We will point out the practical advantages and disadvantages of living together. We will show you the options available when purchasing property together, and how the IRS views spousal equivalents.   We will introduce you to the concept of the cohabitation agreement, and discuss wills, estate and financial planning and medical powers of attorney.

In short, we will show you how to protect yourself and your partner, not from each other, but from the real world and its notable lack of protections for spousal equivalents.

We have attempted to point out pitfalls and present a variety of options for all unmarried couples. If you live with someone in a domestic relationship, or if you're thinking about moving in together, this advice can be invaluable.

The information presented in these pages, by necessity, is general in nature. Just as a doctor can't diagnose you over the phone, an attorney and an accountant can't identify all the symptoms that your particular situation may have.

Let this guide be a starting point. Then consult an attorney, accountant or financial planner of your choice to apply this information to the practical issues in your own relationship.

JUST LIVING TOGETHER? 1

Marriage is a great institution, but I'm not ready for an institution.

Mae West

All couples seek love, sexual and emotional satisfaction, and trust. The social change of the last few decades has allowed many couples to look for the fulfillment of these goals in relationships outside of marriage. Today, cohabitation of opposite sex couples does not attract the disapproval it once did, and same sex couples are finding they have more options than ever before.

However, when a couple moves in together, practical problems inevitably tag along in the wake of romance. Dealing with these problems is bad enough, without being bogged down in the technical terms that the legal and financial communities use to obscure solutions to everyday issues.

In the next few pages, four fictional couples will be introduced to illustrate the variety of situations spousal equivalents may encounter. The challenges each of these couples face in their relationships will serve as examples in the following chapters to illustrate both ordinary and extraordinary situations and their solutions.

A yuppie couple

William and Mary have been living together in Dallas for about a year. William is 38; Mary is 35. Both are divorced.

Mary has been single for six years and has spent the time casually dating and building up a computer company. She married her college sweetheart and, after a few years, found that they had just drifted apart. She has no children.

William is a stockbroker and has been with the same firm since he finished his master's degree. His wife filed for divorce because she was bored with the marriage, and the divorce became final only a month before he met Mary. He has a five year old son who lives with his ex-wife.

The couple dated for approximately fourteen months after meeting in a professional singles group. As they found themselves spending more and more time together, it became obvious that, as busy urban professionals, the amount of time spent "dating" and commuting was counter-productive. Mary brought up the subject of living together one workday morning when William was driving her back to her apartment and she was running late. William had been thinking the same thing, but had not gotten around to bringing it up. He agreed that it would make perfect sense for Mary to move into his townhouse.

The psychic wounds of William's divorce were still healing when he first met Mary, and the financial beating continues. Although Texas courts cannot order alimony, William agreed to pay his ex-wife contractual alimony in order to protect his retirement and pension funds. He agreed to pay a sum equal to her 1/2 interest in these assets over a four year period, and he also pays approximately 20% of his net pay in child support. Effectively, he actually brings home about half of his earnings.

Since Mary is self-employed, it is difficult to estimate her income. Her primary priority is her business, and most of her profits are re-invested in her company. William, even after his other obligations, still seems to have more disposable income than Mary does. They have agreed to have a maid once a week, but Mary is willing to do the majority of the household chores in return for William contributing slightly more to the kitty each month.

A same sex couple

William has an older brother named Bob. Bob, 42, is a surgeon who lives with his boyfriend, Ted, in San Francisco. Ted, 31, is an artist who is still struggling but has occasional financial successes which have allowed him to continue his career. William is aware that his brother lives with Ted and, although they do not discuss the arrangement, has offered his tacit understanding and acceptance to the relationship.

Bob and Ted, who met through mutual friends, have lived together for about five years. They travel frequently, entertain often and live a first-class lifestyle full of fascinating friends and places. Ted, obviously, does not bring in the money that Bob does. However, Bob has substantial real estate holdings and Ted has been the guiding force behind renovating and maintaining these properties. His artistic talents are largely responsible for the profits that Bob realizes from these investments.

An older couple

Mary's father, Nick, lives in a small community where Mary grew up. He retired after a lifetime with a large oil company, and receives a comfortable pension and social security check each month. Although he does not have a sizeable estate, he owns his own home and has enough to travel occasionally. His wife died about five years ago after a long illness. Nick found himself single after nearly forty years and learned that an unmarried man of his age could still be in demand. One night he met a woman named Nora at a dance and they began dating.

Nick is 66; Nora is 57.   Nora works as a receptionist at a dentist's office.   When she was 52, and living in Michigan, her husband announced one morning that he was divorcing her and marrying his 25 year old secretary. Nora had devoted herself to raising her three children and being an accomplished homemaker and hostess for her husband, who ran his family business. At age 53, she moved back to Texas to be near her sister and finish raising her children. She also took her first job outside the home. Although she has a college degree, she had never held a paying job.

Nora still receives a modest alimony check each month, but her child support recently stopped when her last child turned 18. As soon as her son left for college, she moved out of her apartment and into Nick's house. With all three of her children in college, she was happy to save the money.

Nora contacted the attorney who handled her divorce and asked him how living with Nick would affect her alimony. He told her that courts are divided on the issue of terminating alimony because of cohabitation, although usually remarriage will end such payments. He said that more and more attorneys are drafting divorce decrees which terminate alimony because of cohabitation. As is the situation with many areas of law affecting spousal equivalents, this is still a gray area.

The attorney also told her that he has several clients who are widowed and have chosen not to marry the men they live with because they would lose their widow's benefits which accrue from their previous marriage. He advises these clients to keep all their assets separate so that there is question that they have no financial responsibility for each other, which can be very important for senior citizens when issues regarding Social Security benefits and Medicaid arise.

He also told her about his own grandmother, who married late in life and was astute enough to have her grandson draw up a pre-marital agreement. However, when her elderly husband later suffered a stroke and applied for Medicaid, they were told that the government doesn't care about pre-marital agreements, and he was denied benefits. His grandmother was left with no option but to cover her new husband's medical expenses out of her first husband's estate, which she had promised she would protect so that it could be left to their grandchildren.

After hearing these stories, Nick and Nora decided they were every happier with their arrangement than before. Nora helps Nick by paying for half of the utilities and food, but he pays the insurance and taxes on the house and pays for their travel and entertainment. They have also vowed to keep their finances separate.

A college couple

All of Nora's children receive student aid, which pays the majority of their tuition. Their father put himself through college and refuses to help with their expenses so that the children can "build character." Nora's middle daughter is named Pat, and she is a junior at a state college in Illinois. Pat has been dating a guy named Mike since she was a freshman in high school, and she chose to move back to Illinois to go to college with him. They have lived together since he started work on his master's degree in her sophomore year.

Mike supposedly lives in a garage apartment for a minimal amount of rent with four roommates and no telephone. Actually, they live in Pat's apartment in a small complex where they receive a rent reduction by operating as on-site managers. Pat uses this extra money and the need for privacy to study to justify to her mom why she doesn't need a roommate. Nora accepts the story and, although both sets of parents suspect that the kids are living together, everyone is more comfortable not confronting the issue.

"Why don't they just get married?"

These couples and other spousal equivalents have found plenty of reasons to "just live together":

♥ Because they take marriage at least as seriously, if not more so, than married people do;

♥ Because two can live as cheaply as one;

♥ Because the benefits of marriage vs. the distressing statistical probabilities of divorce have even odds;

♥ Because living apart doesn't make sense, but they want to stop short of burning all of their bridges;

♥ To find out if they **can**, i.e. a test under conditions of lower risk;

♥ It seems to be the next logical step in a relationship;

♥ Because the legal responsibilities of the state's marriage contract put too great a financial burden on the relationship;

♥ Commitmentphobia;

♥ Dating is idealized and doesn't deal with the ability to determine how he's going to act when he finds that you're out of toothpaste or how she's going to act when you've left the toilet seat up;

♥ Because the archaic rules of some employers do not allow married couples to work for the same organization;

♥ As Winston Churchill once said, "Success is going from failure to failure with no lack of enthusiasm."

♥   Because, as a woman, financial security is not your first priority in a relationship;

♥   Because marriage may be sacred, but that doesn't mean the IRS won't tax it, or that other governmental agencies won't find ways to interfere in personal financial arrangements;

♥   Because sometimes divorce takes a long time to negotiate;

♥   Because same sex couples are not permitted by law to enter into a legal marriage;

♥   Because a private commitment is more important than a public one;

♥   Or because they know that the question "Why don't you just get married?" will turn into "When are you going to have kids?"

Whatever the reasons, William and Mary, et al, are only a few examples of the growing numbers who have chosen cohabitation as a lifestyle. The patterns of our intimate associations have undergone drastic changes in the past two decades. What is responsible for this POSSLQ explosion?

Don't Marry, Be Happy.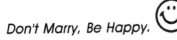
Popular T-shirt slogan

At one time in our history, living together without benefit of marriage was considered "deviant" behavior and criminal laws were enacted to discourage it. Today, unstructured domestic unions composed of both opposite sex and same sex couples are widespread, and some demographers predict that the ever increasing numbers will eventually make cohabitation the majority experience.

One reason for the dramatic increase in spousal equivalents is a sharp decline in social disapproval of cohabitation and the virtual removal of the legal stigma of illegitimacy. Consider the number of contemporary actresses who are not married to the father of their children and compare the acceptance of their liaisons with the public outcry against Ingrid Bergman when she had a child out of wedlock only thirty odd years ago.

The vast majority of the thirtysomething generation may have grown up in traditional families, but they don't live in them today. The baby–boom generation broke through a lot of barriers, for better or worse, and paved the way for those younger **and** older to choose cohabitation as a viable lifestyle.

How many spousal equivalents are there?

In the 1980 census, approximately 1.8 million Americans reported that they were living with a member of the opposite sex without the benefit of marriage. This figure was a 300% increase over the findings of the 1970 census. To categorize this phenomenon, the Census Bureau coined the phrase "Persons of the Opposite Sex Sharing Living Quarters." This unwieldy mouthful was reduced to the acronym "POSSLQ."

Considering the underreporting of many minority groups and illegal aliens and the reluctance of those receiving alimony or government benefits to admit to such an arrangement, educated guesses on the number of POSSLQ's nationwide are as high as 8 million. And these numbers do not even begin to include the millions of same sex couples who share living quarters.

Other surveys confirm that cohabitation is widespread. A nationwide survey conducted by the University of Wisconsin in Madison revealed that nearly half of all Americans in their thirties have, at one time, lived with a person of the opposite sex outside of marriage.

Sociologists Larry Bumpass and James Sweet interviewed 7,491 randomly selected participants for their Wisconsin survey, and presented these findings at a meeting in New Orleans of the Population Association of America. They found that eleven percent of those surveyed who had married between the years 1965 and 1974 had cohabitated outside marriage.

However, for those married between 1980 and 1984, the figure was an astonishing 44 percent.

The increase in cohabitation is not limited to America, but is truly an international phenomenon. For example, in Sweden, where pressure to marry is not as strong as in the U.S., studies have shown that approximately 30% of the women cohabit. The fact that women are encouraged to work in male-dominated fields and child-care is subsidized may account for the larger numbers. It is estimated that the rate of increase in cohabitation in our country is similar to that in the Netherlands, Finland, Norway and Denmark.

Why do so many people just live together?

What do all these figures mean? Despite the difficulties inherent in reaching accurate statistics, it is clear that the number of cohabitants is increasing rapidly. The results of the 1990 census will undoubtedly show that the trend is continuing.

In our modern society, there has been a frustrating lack of permanence in our relationships. In fact, the concept of permanence has almost been eliminated from the definition of marriage. One of every two marriages ends in divorce and the average length of a marriage before divorce is only five years.

But the need to be part of a couple is a basic human trait. It is strong enough that most people, upon failure of one relationship, will try again. The couple is the unit society is built on—a unit of emotional and economic ties necessary for continuation of the species.

So what are the factors that have led to the instability of our traditional relationships in the first place? In our society, the formation of families was always eased by the opportunities this country offered. Couples were able to marry young, and no longer needed the "extended families" which might have been an economic necessity in the old country. This new freedom meant that romantic love, not practicality, was the basis for marriage until death do us part.

But the Industrial Revolution began to change things. Men were drawn away from the farms, and families became less insular. The Second World War continued the trend as women entered the work force in droves. Their new status as wage earners led women to a re-evaluation of their legal status.

Traditionally, a married woman was incapable of entering into a contract of her own or of acquiring or disposing of property without her husband's consent. Her legal existence was virtually merged into that of her husband, and was totally subordinate to the head of the household. Her status was almost one of servant, and it was her duty to perform domestic duties appropriate to her station without compensation.

Once women began to question their legal status as wives, things would never be the same. These seeds of change took decades to blossom but, coupled with the following factors, blossom they did:

♥   The Pill;

♥   Urbanization;

♥ Continued changes in the traditional roles of the sexes;

♥ A rise in the percentage of the population pursuing a college education, leading to later marriages;

♥ "The marriage squeeze" due to the discrepancy in the male/female ratio;

♥ Studies that show marriage creates happier and healthier husbands than bachelorhood, but show that single women are happier and healthier than wives;

♥ The continued recognition of the legal rights of illegitimate children and the lessening of prejudice towards them.

These factors have led us to a society whose families are in a state of flux. Parties of both sexes began to feel a natural reluctance to be bound by legal ties in a relationship that the odds predicted would only be temporary. The aversion to endowing "all my worldly goods" became understandable, especially to those who had experienced the trauma and expense of a prior marriage. Alimony might last a lifetime for these refugees from the marital wars, even if the relationship did not.

What are the results of the POSSLQ Explosion?

The good news for spousal equivalents is that the National Center for Health Statistics surveyed 7,969 women and found that unmarried couples who live together have sex more often than either married couples or singles.

The bad news is the unromantic truth that singles who live together lack many legal and financial advantages that married couples enjoy.

Unmarried couples fight many of the same battles as married couples, but with fewer models to guide them. Unrestricted by marital traditions, spousal equivalents must make up their own rules as they go along, attempting to find their own answers to the common questions which confront all couples today.

Don't let ignorance of the complicated new set of rules of the game stand in your way. The law has not kept up with the changes in our lifestyles. This book will show you how to protect yourself until it does.

"There is nothing new under the sun."

King Solomon

To understand the contemporary position taken by our courts and legislatures towards spousal equivalents, a survey of the historical status of unmarried couples is invaluable.   Society must continually challenge and interpret its laws to fit the needs of citizens.   And there is no area where this is more true or hits closer to home than "family law."

"Free Unions"

The idea and acceptance of "free unions" is as old as ancient Greece. No less an authority than historian Will Durant has estimated that these liaisons outnumbered legal marriages in the first century after that country's golden age.   Under the oldest legal system recorded, the Code of Hammurabi in ancient Babylon, contractual or legal marriage was reserved for the monied classes only, leaving the vast majority of that society in unstructured relationships.

The legal fiction of the informal marriage

Much of our justice system in the United States is derived from the unwritten "common law" of England.

This system of jurisprudence bases its decisions on precedents established in the courts rather than strict legislative rules. Common law is distinct from "civil law," which is a descendant of the Roman law system in many western countries.

The basic theory of common law was that broad principles of justice and reason were determined by the social needs of the community and adapted to new conditions as society required. Practical and sensible laws in everyday usage were often well-established by the time they were actually codified by statute.

In 1753, the passage of Lord Hardwicke's Act in England proclaimed that marriage must be solemnized publicly so that society had a memorable event and the creation of a permanent record. These formal, ceremonial marriages established a legal relationship with specific rights and duties between two people.

Early settlers in America, however, had a problem following Lord Hardwicke's rules. Finding someone to formalize a marriage and somewhere to record it was not easy. There were much longer distances between communities here than in England and, often, roads were inadequate. The early settlers were frequently uneducated and unfamiliar with the law. These factors, as well as a lack of established local government, made a more informal alternative necessary.

As a result of the applications of common law principles, the legal recognition of informal, or common-law, marriages became widespread. When competent parties agreed to form a relationship and live together as husband and wife without a ceremony, the law adapted to acknowledge that a marriage had been created. These informal marriages conferred the same legal status and consequences on the parties as if a public solemnization and recording had taken place.

As the country began to grow, though, local governments enacted more laws. The public became better educated and less hampered by transportation problems. The need for "proof" of the intentions of the parties in informal relationships and the possibility of fraudulent claims led many states away from this trend.

Gradually, governments began to deny the right of two people to enter into their own form of "marriage." The courts and legislatures took the position that only traditional families should be promoted by the laws; any alternative was viewed as a means to undermine the stability of marriage and family life.

Today, a few states continue to recognize the existence of informal or common-law marriage. These include Alabama, Colorado, Georgia, Idaho, Iowa, Kansas, Montana, New Hampshire, Ohio, Oklahoma, Pennsylvania, Rhode Island, South Carolina, Texas and the District of Columbia. Utah, in an unusual twist, did not just keep the law on the books, but actually passed a statute in 1987 permitting common-law marriage.

Most states will recognize an informal marriage if it was originally contracted in one of these states. The impact of these contemporary laws on spousal equivalents will be discussed at length in the next chapter.

The "putative spouse" doctrine

Although the majority of the states moved away from granting legal status to those couples outside a ceremonial marriage, there have long been protections for innocent victims of bigamists or void marriages, where a "putative spouse" was under the mistaken view that a marriage existed. Examples of void marriages would be situations where (a) one party was underage, (b) marriage was against the law because of a family relationship between the parties, or (c) a waiting period after a divorce was not observed.

Many of the protections for putative spouses remain today. The doctrine was enacted to protect a good faith party who was entitled to a share of accumulated property. An innocent "spouse" who could prove ignorance of a marriage impediment would be protected by the courts.

It's a Crime to Live Together

Few protections remained, however, for those who lived together with knowledge of the illegal or immoral nature of their relationship. As the perceived necessity for informal marriage decreased, the laws changed to such an extent that it became a crime to live together in virtually every state.

It is worthy of note that, although only open and notorious sexual conduct outside of marriage was deemed offensive to the public at common law, some of these laws remain on the books. Laws against nonmarital cohabitation still exist in Arizona, Florida, Idaho, Illinois, Michigan, Mississippi, New Mexico, North Carolina, North Dakota, Virginia, and West Virginia. As a practical matter, these laws are rarely enforced, and the constitutionality of these statutes continues to be called into question. Spousal equivalents should write their legislators to inform them that these archaic laws need to be repealed.

Meretricious relationships

Along with the criminal laws, a virtually unanimous legal view arose that couples who lived together did so at their own peril and could not rely on a court to endorse their illicit living arrangements. The adjective "meretricious" (defined in Webster's as "of or relating to a prostitute" as it is based on the Latin word meretrix, meaning prostitute) became a legal term for couples who cohabitated without following Lord Hardwicke's rules.

As a result, anyone bold enough to voice the term "contract" in connection with the word "sex" in a courtroom was not met with sympathy. In fact, such claims were denied on the basis of a widespread legal position which limited the right of people "living in sin" to even form a contract.

The right to contract freely with the expectation that the contract will be upheld is as fundamental in our society as the right to write and speak without restraint. But the courts have always taken the position that they could refuse to enforce an otherwise valid contract because it was against public policy.

The term "public policy" is inherently vague. In an effort to define the term, the courts have repeatedly held that they would not enforce contracts that either injure the public welfare or are contrary to public decency, sound policy and good morals.

Agreements which violate public policy include such examples as gambling contracts, murder for hire contracts, or agreements in restraint of trade. Unmarried couples who lived together and attempted to form a contract were likely to find themselves in this category. In the few cases when the courts did seek to enact justice when one cohabitant brought suit against another, they were only able to do so by finding a way to equate cohabitation with marriage.

The laws adapt

But as society changes its economic and social makeup, public policy interests must also change. The problem facing the courts today is how to determine when public interests have changed so much that the old rules become obsolete.

One of the difficulties in making these decisions is that judges in different parts of the country are as likely to have different perspectives on interpretation of situations as judges in different periods of time. This inconsistency has led many legal commentators to focus on the need for legislative action to protect cohabitants, with proposals that an interest in jointly acquired property be a matter of statute rather than contract. But with fifty different legislative bodies, this solution is still a conflict-ridden process.

So the law remains in a constant state of flux. As traditional ideas of family change, the courts and legislatures find themselves preparing to meet the new demands for laws which protect the alternative families which exist in the real world.

CONTEMPORARY APPROACHES   4

There is only one thing about which I am certain, and that is that there is very little about which one can be certain.
                          W. Somerset Maugham

Significant changes in the law often begin with a landmark case. For spousal equivalents, the legal vacuum ended in 1976 when the *Marvin vs. Marvin* case, called one of the most misunderstood decisions of modern times, was decided by the Supreme Court of California. The lawsuit involving the Oscar-winning actor Lee Marvin and his live-in girlfriend introduced the word "palimony" into the language.

Before *Marvin*, the law took a two-prong approach to the dilemma of unmarried cohabitation:

1. The courts found a way to pretend the relationship was a marriage; or

2. The courts denied any rights at all to "meretricious" couples.

The Impact of Marvin vs. Marvin

The *Marvin* case, which will be discussed in depth later in this chapter, added a third alternative for the

legal system to consider as they pondered the rights of
spousal equivalents:

   3. The courts could admit such a
      relationship wasn't a marriage, but apply
      equitable principles to prevent hardship
      and injustice to a spousal equivalent.

   Equitable principles provide remedies for those in
unjust situations. "Equity" can be defined as "justice."
When strict adherence to rigid rules in England
appeared to yield an unfair result, the King established
courts of chancery to do what was just and right when
the common law failed. This idea has always been
incorporated in the American legal system. Common-
law marriage and the putative spouse doctrine are alike
in that they are also based on theories of equity.
   Many of the emerging theories on cohabitation,
which seek to overturn the old order of discrimination
against "meretricious" relationships, are based on these
same principles. The changes in the laws which affect
spousal equivalents, for better or for worse, have been
inspired by creative attorneys who chose to challenge
the legal status quo, usually to protect the claims of
women. That's what got Lee Marvin in trouble.
   So what would be the anticipated result today if a
spousal equivalent tried to take a case to court? Which
of the three legal alternatives can be expected?

Informal Marriages Today

   One of the basic assumptions of this book is that
spousal equivalents want to avoid the first legal
alternative. Therefore, it is important to be aware of

the laws regarding informal, or common-law, marriage if you live in a state which still recognizes this relationship.

One of the modern day reasons for retaining such a legal status has been the protection of children, since many states did not recognize paternity suits until forced to by the Supreme Court in 1973. Prior to these laws, construing a live-in relationship as a marriage was the only way the states could order fathers to support their offspring.

Even the jurisdictions which recognize informal marriage today are often critical of this legal anachronism. There are plenty of public officials to perform marriage ceremonies and there are plenty of clerks willing to record the marriage licenses. The chances are that a couple who wants to get married won't even encounter transportation problems.

It used to be that society afforded this protection to those on the lower rungs of the socio-economic ladder. But in our changing times, those who really need protection are those on the higher rungs of that ladder who, for whatever reason, haven't formalized their union, and have the deep pockets to make a lawsuit worth fighting.

As was the case with the lawsuit against Lee Marvin, celebrities seem to be the ones who focus media attention on such issues and bring them to the attention of the public. Recently, actor William Hurt and major league baseball's Dave Winfield have been slapped with claims of common-law marriage, making people aware that this is not an outmoded idea whose time has come and gone.

It is a common misconception that the length of cohabitation creates common-law status. This is not true: there must be an agreement between the parties to be married and a "holding-out" (representing yourself as husband and wife) in the community before this legal fiction is created. Signing leases as husband and wife or filing joint tax returns are examples of proof of common-law marriages. Appendix A in the back of this book will explain the laws which exist in your home state.

If you are concerned that you and your spousal equivalent may have created an informal marriage, contact an attorney. If you have complied with the requirements, the law is clear. A common-law marriage is the full equivalent of a ceremonial marriage, and a divorce is required to dissolve the relationship.

The second legal alternative is still a reality. But let's discuss the good news first.

"Palimony"

Lee Marvin may have been an award-winning actor, but his name was immortalized when famous (since then) divorce lawyer Marvin Mitchelson filed suit against him and created the concept of "palimony."

Most recently, Clint Eastwood and Rod Stewart have found themselves in similar situations, when live-in lovers filed suit for a share of the money earned during their years together. In between these two cases, celebrities such as Billie Jean King, Nick Nolte, Frank Serpico, Peter Frampton, Alice Cooper, Flip Wilson, and Rod Steiger have also faced lawsuits filed by former spousal equivalents.

Despite the negative connotations of the word "palimony", the *Marvin* case was actually a long-

awaited recognition of the live-in lifestyle from one of
the most influential courts in the country.

This historical event began in 1964 when Michelle
Triola (who later legally changed her name to Marvin)
met Lee Marvin on a movie set in Hollywood. Michelle
was recovering from a divorce; by all accounts, Lee was
sleeping in his dressing room as he was beginning one.

After that, many versions of the events that
transpired are available. Michelle's story was that Lee,
although never promising to marry her, did agree that
they would hold themselves out in public as husband
and wife. He promised to support her for the rest of
her life if she would devote herself to his demands for
full-time companionship, and give up her career.
Faced with this decision, she chose Lee.

Then came the night when he called from Las
Vegas and told her he had tied the knot with a new
Mrs. Marvin. Shortly after that, she was evicted from
the spacious home in Malibu that they had shared.
Eighteen months later, the monthly check he had been
sending also stopped.

The lower courts weren't impressed by Michelle's
plight. They applied the second legal alternative to the
case to this "meretricious" couple, and they had
tradition on their side.

But, on appeal, the justices of the Supreme Court
of California began to wade into the legal mire of rights
and duties of spousal equivalents, unafraid to go where
no court had gone before. They had their eyes wide
open.

In a realistic, unprecedented statement, the court
admitted that "the mores of the society have indeed
changed so radically in regard to cohabitation that we
cannot impose a standard based on alleged moral
considerations that have apparently been so widely

abandoned by so many." They also took the even-handed opinion that "concepts of 'guilt' ... cannot justify an unequal division of property between two equally 'guilty' persons."

Although reserving the old notion that agreements between nonmarital partners fail to the extent that they are based only on meretricious sexual services, the justices decided that "in the absence of an express contract, the courts should inquire into the conduct of the parties to determine whether that conduct demonstrates an implied contract, agreement of partnership or joint venture, or some other tacit understanding between the parties. The courts may also employ the doctrine of quantum meruit, or equitable remedies such as constructive or resulting trusts, when warranted by the facts of the case."

English, please

What do these theories of recovery mean in everyday English?

Contracts

Basically, a contract is an oral or written agreement. There must be an offer, acceptance and consideration for a contract to have enforceable legal rights. The offer and acceptance parts are clear enough, and consideration merely means the transfer of something of value, i.e. cash, services, etc.

An express contract is one that is actually stated or committed to writing, (and therefore can be either written or oral). An implied contract is inferred from the conduct of the parties.

Quantum meruit

The equitable principles of quantum meruit and constructive and resulting trusts were also brought up in the opinion. The Latin term quantum meruit loosely translated means "for what it's worth." For spousal equivalents, this theory could apply when one party performs valuable services for the other and those services are accepted and enjoyed in circumstances which would lead the receiving party to realize that something was expected in return.

Constructive and Resulting Trusts

A trust is a right in property which is held by one party for the benefit of another. A resulting trust arises when it appears from the transaction that this was the intent of the parties. A constructive, or involuntary, trust is found to exist to prevent the unjust enrichment of the one holding the property. A resulting trust involves intent, but a constructive trust can be found contrary to the intent of the parties when justice requires such a finding.

The Results of Marvin vs. Marvin

The outcome for Michelle Triola Marvin was not a bright one, however. After the ground-breaking findings of the appeal court, the case was remanded back to the lower courts for a new trial.

Though she originally sought $1.6 million, on re-trial of the case Michelle was awarded $104,000 as rehabilitative alimony. This award was later overturned on appeal, and Michelle received nothing.

The principles had been established, but Michelle's battle was futile. The final verdict: the facts of her case failed to meet any of the criteria the court had established.

But the *Marvin* decision recognized the capacity of unmarried couples to contract between themselves, and stated that the courts had the power to determine a division of the property of spousal equivalents according to "their reasonable expectations." The case was a great start. But spousal equivalents should not be lulled into a false sense of security by the high-sounding legal theories the judges quoted. The specter of legal alternative number two is still with us. The *Marvin* case was decided nearly fifteen years ago and many younger spousal equivalents may never have heard of the late actor, much less the case itself. Since that time, the legal community has certainly not blindly lined up behind the California justices.

Hewitt vs. Hewitt

The 1978 Hewitt case came out of Illinois, a notably less progressive state than California. The scenario in this case involves a dentist, a woman he introduced as his wife for fifteen years, and their three children.

Victoria Hewitt lived with Robert Hewitt from 1960 to 1975. As college students in 1960, after discovering parenthood was imminent, they announced to their parents that they had gotten married (despite the fact that there had been no ceremony). From that time on, Victoria and Robert held themselves out to the rest of the world as husband and wife.

Robert told Victoria that he would "share his life, his future, his earnings and his property" with her. Based on these promises, she devoted her wifely efforts to his professional education as a dentist and, thereafter, to the establishment of his practice of pedodontia. She even borrowed money from her parents to help his career.

Victoria worked for Robert in his office, but the paycheck she received was put into a joint account. Robert's practice flourished and he went from impoverished student to $80,000 a year professional by 1975. During the fifteen years of their relationship, he became a prominent dentist with significant accumulated property.

Victoria, meanwhile, had borne three children and dedicated herself to being wife, mother, and helpmate in her husband's career, including coordinating social activities required to enhance his professional reputation.

But then Robert decided to leave Victoria. Despite an appeals court finding that she was entitled to the rights and privileges of a spouse, the Illinois Supreme Court proceeded to conclude that the so-called Mrs. Hewitt had no rights whatsoever. They held that her claim was unenforceable as it "contravened public policy."

There is no recognition of common-law marriage in Illinois. Because the court viewed itself as the watchdog of society, whose duty it was to "strengthen and preserve the integrity of marriage and safeguard family relationships," it refused to grant legal status to a private arrangement which sought to substitute itself for legal marriage.

The court further found that the question of change in the laws governing the rights of spousal equivalents involved the evaluation of information that was best suited to "investigative and fact-finding facilities of (the) legislative branch in exercise of its traditional authority to declare public policy in (the) domestic relations field."

Victoria was left holding the proverbial bag, and was denied a division of their accumulated property.

Alexander vs. Alexander

A similar result was reached in a 1984 case in Mississippi. Margie Alexander lived with Sam Alexander for approximately thirty years until his death. Margie, apparently in ignorance of the fact that she could obtain a divorce from a husband who had deserted her, lived with Sam although legally married to another.

Margie shared Sam's name, assets and liabilities. During the last twenty years of his life, they lived in a house they paid for together, although the title was in Sam's name only.

Sam's two sisters and two nephews were his legal heirs because he did not leave a will. They wanted Margie out of Sam's house. Margie felt she had a right to stay in the home she had helped to buy.

Without an agreement of any kind between Sam and Margie, the court agreed with the relatives. Margie's years as "faithful spouse" were not enough absent any showing that she expected compensation for her services. Besides, the judges said, if Sam had wanted Margie to have the house, he would have drawn up a will or made some other arrangements before he died.

The court quoted from the *Hewitt* case, as well as the *Carnes vs. Sheldon* case out of Michigan. In this case, the theory behind a denial of rights to a spousal equivalent was that, although the judicial branch had the power to fashion remedies, to do so would resurrect common-law marriage.

A more realistic approach was taken by a judge who dissented in Margie's case.   He said that "occasionally, a court's well-intentioned efforts to see that a rule of law is promoted results in principles of justice being ignored. The inequity which results from the majority's opinion makes it evident that this is one of those instances...I must respectfully, but adamantly dissent."

Although the lower court had given Margie an equitable lien on the home in an effort to allow her to live there, the relatives got the house after the appeals court finished with the case.

Don't Roll the Dice

Although courts and lawmakers historically have balked at conveying the rights and benefits of marriage to non-married couples, the argument in favor of doing just that is the same as the argument against. In the promotion of marriage and the family by the state, coupled with their concern for social productivity and stability, it seems society's best interest would be served by recognizing a stable, marriage-like relationship. Isn't the nature of the relationship more important than its formal registration?

Certainly, efforts in the past to discourage cohabitation have not led to a decrease in the numbers opting for this lifestyle, nor a return to traditional family structures. Until the laws begin to offer more protection, spousal equivalents who neglect to make provisions for each other in the event of death or dissolution of the relationship are gambling with their futures.

What happened to Victoria and Margie can happen to you if you let romance blind you to reality. Spousal equivalents with deep pockets run the risk of the opposite result: a court sympathetic to the financially dependent party.   Only a written cohabitation agreement provides the protection both sides need.

COHABITATION AGREEMENTS   5

A verbal contract isn't worth the paper it's written on.
Samuel Goldwyn

What is a Cohabitation Agreement?

There are no protections for the spousal equivalent upon the death or disability of a partner. There are few protections for the spousal equivalent upon dissolution of the relationship. When signing a premarital agreement, often you are merely protecting yourself from each other. A cohabitation agreement will protect both of you from the outside world.

The need for preparation of a will and preparation of a cohabitation agreement are very similar. Regardless of what state you live in, if you don't have a written contract, it is possible the court now has the right to determine a division of your property according to what they believe is fair. This is vague, yes, but the only guideline there is at this point. At least you can be sure without a will where your money (or at least what's left of it) will go. If you don't have a cohabitation agreement, there's no guaranteed fall-back position.

Also, consider the consequences if one spousal equivalent is sued by a creditor or audited by the IRS.

A cohabitation agreement proves what is what and whose is whose in no uncertain terms.

Cohabitation agreements for same sex couples are even more important. Just as the law has often refused to deal with opposite sex couples who cohabited because of their "so-called" bad faith, same sex couples have run the risk of being jailed for "immoral conduct." For those couples who have not gone public, risking publicity and exposure by filing a lawsuit has often outweighed the potential benefits.

Moving in together is a leap of faith, but don't let it be a blind one. Consider a cohabitation agreement. At no time should "if you loved me, you wouldn't need me to sign an agreement" enter into the equation. Trust and love should not be compromised by practical considerations. The duration of your cohabitation, details of your sexual relations, personal finances, and services rendered are not details most people want revealed to the world.

Elements of Cohabitation Agreements

The law affecting cohabitation agreements is new and continually evolving. There are substantial restrictions imposed on premarital, postmarital and separation agreements by the courts. The application of these same standards to cohabitation agreements is to be expected.

To guarantee that the courts take such a contract seriously, a cohabitation agreement must be in writing and signed by both parties. To be enforceable, it is necessary that a contract be negotiated "at arm's length." Simply, one party gives something to the other expecting something in return, in a situation where there is no fraud, with neither taking advantage of the other.

These elements become even more critical in a confidential relationship. To be safe, there must be full and fair disclosure of all relevant information. If these steps aren't followed, charges of fraud, conflict of interest, misrepresentation, or overreaching by a trusted partner can void the agreement.

Hand in hand with full disclosure, the agreement must be entered into voluntarily, without duress or coercion. Any provisions which are oppressive to one spousal equivalent would be automatically suspect to any judge reviewing the contract.

It is easy to see this is not just a matter of who gets what. To avoid any of these potential problems, it is critical that both parties hire their own counsel to prepare and review the document. If only one attorney is involved in the process, the court is likely to uphold any claims of fraud or duress.

The validity and enforceability of your agreement depend on all these factors. Not covering all the bases could mean that you are wasting your time and money. The glut of do-it-yourself books on the market is dangerous, as these books may be out of date by the time it rolls off the presses. But attorneys must keep up with the law on an almost day-to-day basis. A consultation with the attorney of your choice would determine recent changes which affect any of the advice in this book, as well.

More than half the states in the country have expressly stated that they will recognize and enforce these agreements between spousal equivalents. Only three states have said they will not: Georgia, Illinois, and Louisiana. The obstacles in these states remain the same: the protection of marital relationships and the objection to enforcing immoral agreements. (See Appendix A for the legal position of your home state.)

Once you understand how your state has viewed spousal equivalents in the past, take a conservative approach when you execute your own agreement. A creative approach, while it may change the law as Michelle Triola Marvin did, might not help your particular situation.

Think and act preventively. An agreement to live together may be the last thing you want, but it is easily the first thing the cautious spousal equivalent needs.

Sample Cohabitation Agreement

The following agreement is an example only. No two cohabitation agreements will be alike and this agreement is included here only to give you an idea of the issues to cover.

The following chapters will address the pertinent issues to be covered in your own cohabitation agreement in further depth, and explain your options in greater detail. We have used William and Mary as an example in this agreement, but the agreement would be valid for a same sex couple as well.

Chapter 13 will provide a checklist for determining your own needs, and give you information on how to choose an attorney to prepare your cohabitation agreement.

COHABITATION AGREEMENT
BETWEEN
WILLIAM SMITH AND MARY JONES

This agreement is made by and between **WILLIAM SMITH** hereinafter called "Smith" and **MARY JONES** hereinafter called "Jones," who will be referred to in the agreement as the "partners."

In consideration of the mutual promises contained herein, and with the intention of being bound by this agreement, the partners stipulate and agree as follows:

ARTICLE 1
STIPULATIONS

Cohabitation

Although the partners are not married, they began living together in the same residence on January 1, 1989, and intend to continue this living arrangement.

Marital Status and Residence

Each of the partners is an unmarried person and a permanent resident of Texas.

Occupation

WILLIAM SMITH is a stockbroker with the firm of **Doe and Associates.**

MARY JONES is a computer specialist, and owns and operates her own firm, **Computer Connections**. Her firm is a sole proprietorship, and is, as of the date of this agreement, unincorporated.

Intent of the Partners

It is the desire and intent of the partners that, by entering into this agreement, they will define and clarify their intentions and expectations regarding their financial rights and responsibility to each other, including rights regarding property and support. The partners do not intend that their joint residency create a marital relationship.

Agreement for Continuing Dialogue

To carry out the intent of this agreement, the partners commit themselves to continuing dialogue concerning the rights and duties as set out herein. In the spirit of fairness, the partners agree to attempt to resolve disputes that may arise in the future through compromise.

ARTICLE 2
EFFECTIVE DATES

Effective Dates

This agreement shall be effective May 1, 1990, and will continue until the termination of the cohabitation of the partners or the death of either partner. The cohabitation of the partners may be terminated at any time by either partner.

Marriage of the Partners

It is the mutual intent of the partners that this agreement be deemed an antenuptial agreement and that its terms be given full force and effect in the event of a ceremonial marriage of the partners. The creation of a marriage between the parties must be ceremonial in nature.

ARTICLE 3
PRESENT FINANCIAL STATUS

Present Financial Status

Each partner has carefully examined the other's financial condition and position. Smith represents that the financial statement attached hereto as Exhibit A is a true and accurate statement of his assets and liabilities. Jones represents that the financial statement attached hereto as Exhibit B is a true and accurate statement of her assets and liabilities. Each partner has examined the other's present assets and liabilities as shown on the attached schedules and made all inquiries about the other's assets and liabilities deemed appropriate. Each partner acknowledges receipt of satisfactory information and responses to all such inquiries.

ARTICLE 4
SEPARATE PROPERTY

Assets and Liabilities As Separate Property

The property described will remain the separate property of the partner who is the titleholder, free of any interest, beneficial, equitable, or otherwise, in the other partner:

1. All property, whether real or personal, owned by the respective partner at the effective date of this agreement.

2. All property acquired by the respective partner out of the proceeds or income from property owned at the effective date of this agreement or attributable to appreciation in value of said property, whether the enhancement is due to market conditions or services, skills, or efforts of the owner of the property.

3. All property hereafter acquired by the respective partner by gift, devise, bequest, or inheritance, or income from said property, or attributable to appreciation in value of said property, whether the enhancement is due to market conditions or services, skills, or efforts of the owner of the property.

Earnings As Separate Property

Except as hereinafter provided, the earnings and income of each partner, while the partners are living together and thereafter, will remain his or her separate property, respectively, and will not be subject to division on termination of the relationship.

ARTICLE 5
PROPERTY AND LIABILITIES OF WILLIAM SMITH

Property and Liabilities of WILLIAM SMITH

The property described on Schedule C, attached to this agreement and made a part of it for all purposes, is and will remain the separate property of **WILLIAM SMITH.**

The liabilities and obligations described on Schedule D, attached to this agreement and made a part of it for all purposes, are the sole liabilities and obligations of **WILLIAM SMITH,** to be satisfied and paid solely from his separate estate and from which he will forever hold harmless, indemnify, and defend **MARY JONES** from any claim.

Any taxes, interest, or penalties that **WILLIAM SMITH** may owe for income received or accrued by him or that are otherwise attributable to him are the sole liabilities and obligations of **WILLIAM SMITH,** to be satisfied and paid solely from his separate estate and from which she will forever hold harmless, indemnify, and defend **MARY JONES** from any claims.

ARTICLE 6
PROPERTY AND LIABILITIES OF MARY JONES

Property and Liabilities of MARY JONES

The property described on Schedule E, attached to this agreement and made a part of it for all purposes, is and will remain the separate property of **MARY JONES**.

The liabilities and obligations described on Schedule F, attached to this agreement and made a part of it for all purposes, are the sole liabilities and obligations of **MARY JONES**, to be satisfied and paid solely from her separate estate and from which she will forever hold harmless, indemnify, and defend **WILLIAM SMITH** from any claim.

Any taxes, interest, or penalties that **MARY JONES** may owe for income received or accrued by her or that are otherwise attributable to her are the sole liabilities and obligations of **MARY JONES**, to be satisfied and paid solely from her separate estate and from which she will forever hold harmless, indemnify, and defend **WILLIAM SMITH** from any claim.

ARTICLE 7
LIVING EXPENSES

Provision for Payment of Living Expenses

WILLIAM SMITH will pay sixty percent (60%) and **MARY JONES** will pay forty percent (40%) of their living expenses while they are living together.

Each partner will, from his or her separate funds, defray his or her personal living expenses, pay for his or her purely personal expenses for clothing and otherwise, and maintain or provide for his or her separate property and investments.

Each partner will file his or her own separate income tax returns and will pay his or her individual income taxes from his or her own separate funds.   All property or household goods purchased from any joint account and any balance in any joint account will be owned in the same percentages as contributions to the account.   All banking accounts will be kept separately by the respective partners, and each will maintain his or her other accounts free from commingling of funds.

ARTICLE 8
FUTURE CREDIT TRANSACTIONS

Future Credit Transactions of Partners

As each partner desires to allow the other to enter into credit transactions without his or her approval or joinder or nonjoinder, the partners make the following agreement respecting such future credit transaction. If either partner enters into a transaction wherein credit is extended to that partner or that partner becomes liable or obligated for the repayment, contingent or otherwise, of credit extended to any third party, whether or not the transaction is appropriately denominated as a "separate–property" transaction, and unless a contrary intent is specifically and expressly stated, then that obligation will be satisfied by the partner incurring it wholly from his or her separate property, and the partner incurring the obligation will hold the other partner harmless from that obligation and indemnify him or her if he or she is ever required for any reason to satisfy that obligation. The assets, if any, acquired through any such credit transaction will be and remain the separate property of the partner obligating his or her separate property for the credit extended in acquiring the assets or resulting in the acquisition of the assets. Similarly, any business failure of one of the partners or any bankruptcy, reorganization, composition, arrangement, or other debtor/creditor action of or against a partner will in no way affect the other partner, and neither partner is relying or will rely on the other partner for any credit, accommodation, or indulgence in these regards.

ARTICLE 9
JOINT ASSETS

Acquisition of Joint Assets

The partners may from time to time acquire joint assets by their voluntary act, but no property shall be deemed a joint asset unless it has been so designated by the partners in a written agreement at the time of acquisition. The written instrument shall designate the interest of each with specificity.

ARTICLE 10
DESIGNATION AS BENEFICIARY OF INTERESTS

Life Insurance and Testamentary Bequests

As long as the partners are residing together under the provisions of this agreement, each will maintain the other as a beneficiary of life insurance policies each owns to the extent of Fifty Thousand Dollars ($50,000). In addition, each will maintain the other as a beneficiary under their respective wills to the extent of Ten Thousand Dollars ($10,000). Such designations will be accomplished within thirty days of the signing of this agreement. The failure to name the other party as beneficiary or to execute a will or codicil naming the other party shall create a charge against the estate of the defaulting party in the amount of Ten Thousand Dollars ($10,000) in favor of the party who should have been so designated.

Waiver of Estate Claims

On the death of a partner, whether during the term of this agreement or after its termination, the other party shall not make any claim to any share of interest in the estate of the deceased party except as specifically provided for in this agreement, regardless of whether such interest might be based on a common law or statutory right established before of after the making of this agreement.

No Support Obligations

Nothing in these provisions shall be construed to suggest that either party has undertaken any obligation to support the other beyond what may be expressly provided for in this agreement, nor shall it be construed to suggest that either party intended to leave the other any interest in his or her estate beyond what may be expressly provided for in this agreement.

ARTICLE 11
ARBITRATION

Option to Choose Arbitration

In the event of any dispute over the terms of this Agreement, either partner may invoke binding arbitration by notifying the American Arbitration Association in writing of the issue to be arbitrated with a copy to the other party at their last known address. The partner invoking arbitration shall provide the American Arbitration Association with a copy of the Agreement and pay the American Arbitration Association the fees it requires in order to proceed with arbitration. The arbitrator shall be selected and the arbitration be conducted in accordance with the rules of the American Arbitration Association. The arbitrator shall decide the issues submitted by each party but shall be limited by the terms of the Agreement. The arbitrator shall determine the apportionment of the expenses of the arbitration.

ARTICLE 12
MANAGEMENT, DISPOSITION, AND
TRANSMUTATION OF PROPERTY

Management of Properties

Each partner will have the full, free, and unrestricted right to manage his or her separate property, including, without limitation, the right to convey or encumber that property; to dispose of it by sale, gift, or otherwise; and to deal with it without taking into consideration the other partner.

Dispositions of Property to Other Partner

Notwithstanding any other provision of this agreement, either partner may, only by appropriate, notarized written instrument, transfer, give, convey, devise, or bequeath any property to the other. Neither partner intends by this agreement to limit or restrict in any way the right to receive any such transfer, gift, conveyance, devise, or bequest from the other, except as stated in this agreement.

Transmutation

Except as otherwise provided in this agreement, property or interests in property now owned or hereafter acquired by the partners that by the terms of this agreement are classified as the separate property of one of them can become the separate property of the other or the partners' joint property only by a written instrument executed and acknowledged before a notary public by the partner whose separate property is to be reclassified.

ARTICLE 13
GENERAL PROVISIONS

Benefit and Burden

This agreement will be binding on and inure to the benefit of the partners and their respective heirs, administrators, personal representatives, successors, and assigns.

Consideration for Agreement

The consideration for this agreement is the mutual promise of each partner to act as companion and homemaker to the other, in addition to the other specific promises contained in this agreement. Any services that either partner may provide to the other for the benefit of the other are fully compensated by this agreement.

Fiduciary Duty

Each partner promises to act in good faith and to deal fairly with the other in the management of their joint property in acting under the terms of this agreement.

Support After Separation or Death

Each partner waives the right to be supported by the other after their separation or after the death of either partner, and each partner agrees not to make any claim for such support.

No Intention To Create "Common-Law" or "Informal" Marriage

Neither party will hold himself or herself out as the other party's spouse. The partners are not married at the effective date of this agreement. Neither partner intends to or will do any act or cause any result that will create a factual situation that would create a "common-law marriage" or a presumption in favor of such relationship, an "informal marriage" as defined in sections 1.91 and 1.92 of the Texas Family Code and any cases construing those statutes, or any other public reputation of living together as husband and wife. Any subsequent marriage between the partners must therefore be a formal ceremonial marriage.

Integration

This agreement sets forth the entire agreement between the partners with regard to the subject matter of the agreement. All agreements, covenants, representations, and warranties, express and implied, oral and written, of the partners concerning their financial relationship, past, present, and future, commencing as of the date they began living together and terminating if and when they separate, are contained in this agreement. No other agreements, covenants, representations, or warranties, express or implied, oral or written, have been made by either partner to the other regarding the subject matter of this agreement. All prior and contemporaneous conversations, negotiations, possible and alleged agreements and representations, covenants, and warranties regarding the subject matter of this agreement are waived, merged in the agreement, and superseded by this agreement. This is an integrated agreement.

Severability

If any provision of this agreement is deemed to be invalid or unenforceable, it shall be deemed severable from the remainder of the agreement, which will continue in full force and effect without being impaired or invalidated in any way. If a provision is deemed invalid because of its scope or breadth, it shall be deemed valid to the extent of the scope or breadth permitted by law.

Amendment

This agreement can be amended only by a written agreement signed by both partners in the presence of a notary public.

Governing Law

All rights, duties, and obligations under this agreement are payable and enforceable in Houston, Harris County, Texas. This agreement shall be governed by, and construed and enforced in accordance with, the laws of the state of Texas.

Signing of Agreement

Before signing this agreement, each partner consulted with an attorney of his or her choice, and the terms and legal significance of the agreement and the effect it has on any interest that either partner might accrue in the property of the other were fully explained. Each partner acknowledges that he or she fully understands the agreement and its legal effect, that he or she is signing the agreement freely and voluntarily, and that neither partner has any reason to believe that the other did not fully understand the terms and effects of the agreement or that he or she did not freely and voluntarily execute the agreement.

Interpretation

No provision in this agreement is to be interpreted for or against any partner because that partner or that partner's legal representative drafted the provision.

Costs and Expenses

Each partner will bear their own costs incurred in connection with this agreement, including, without limitation, its negotiation, preparation, and consummation.

Attorney's Fees

If either partner must hire an attorney for the purpose of enforcing or preventing the breach of any provision of this agreement, including, but not limited to, by instituting any action or proceeding to enforce any provision of the agreement, for damages by reason of any alleged breach of any provision of the agreement, for a declaration of that partner's rights or obligations under the agreement, or for any other judicial remedy, then the prevailing partner will be entitled to be reimbursed by the losing partner for all costs and expenses incurred thereby, including, but not limited to, reasonable attorney's fees and costs for the services rendered to the prevailing partner.

(Signature lines of parties and attorneys are also necessary, along with appropriate notarization.)

Chapter 13 will give you specific information on how to decide what to put in your cohabitation agreement and how to choose an attorney to help you prepare the actual document.

Just as a divorce can be obtained on a no-fault basis in most states, the cohabitation agreement is designed so that it does not apportion blame when a relationship ends. The agreement ends when one party moves out, but the enforcement of the agreement is just beginning. If the need arises, a clear, specific agreement will encourage both parties to proceed with a division of their property that is in the spirit of their mutual understandings.

Spousal equivalents who contemplate marriage in the future should not overlook the importance of Article II, *Marriage of the Partners.* The cohabitation agreement can serve the same purpose as a premarital agreement for spousal equivalents who take the plunge.

The cohabitation agreement sets out similar provisions for characterizing property and for its division as would a premarital or prenuptial agreement. However, as this agreement does not meet the criteria of being prepared "in contemplation of marriage," it is wise to use the term "antenuptial" to label your agreement. This would also serve to incorporate its provisions into your marriage contract, unless any provision contravenes the law of your home state.

SPOUSAL EQUIVALENTS AND THE REST OF THE WORLD <u>6</u>

I was married by a judge. I should have asked for a jury.
George Burns

Blood relations, marriage and adoptions legally define families. But it is estimated that fewer than 30% of us live in traditional nuclear families. Over half of new marriages end in divorce. "Yours, mine and ours" blended families are the norm.

As new arrangements leave the law behind, how do we obtain "equal rights" for those who choose to live in non-traditional families?

Married vs. Single

Married people and traditional families take for granted many of the following benefits:

♥ health insurance provided for spouses
   through employers;

♥ an interest in pensions and retirement benefits;

♥ bereavement and sick leave for family members;

♥ moving expenses or unemployment benefits upon relocation of a spouse;

♥ travel packages with reduced rates for family members;

♥ low cost family rates at health clubs, museums, and other private organizations;

♥ living in neighborhoods zoned for single families.

Also taken for granted by married couples are:

♥ filing joint income taxes;

♥ claiming dependency deductions;

♥ visiting family members in hospitals and authorizing their emergency medical treatment;

♥ inheriting from a spouse who dies without a will;

♥ the right to sue for loss of consortium, wrongful death benefits, or workers' compensation benefits;

♥ and the right of privileged communications.

The first tier of benefits listed above are primarily through private organizations and governmental agencies. Spousal equivalents have been granted some of these rights, in some places. Often, simply requesting the policies of a particular company may uncover the fact that they do make special arrangements for spousal equivalents. If not, write a letter asking why it is not possible to receive these benefits. When enough companies hear from enough people, policies change.

Planning for death and disability as well as taxes will each require their own chapter to adequately cover the information spousal equivalents need to know. But the last two benefits are not so easily categorized, and are worthy of at least a brief discussion.

Consortium

The conjugal rights of the marital relationship are many. A spouse's role may be wage–earner, homemaker, companion and lover. When a third party interferes with the ability of one spouse to be any of these things, he deprives the other spouse of the "consortium" of the first. The most common type of interference is the injury or death of a spouse.

Obviously, a spousal equivalent suffers identical damage when a mate is harmed.

The general legal consensus is that an action for loss of consortium is dependent on proof of a valid marriage. Denial of recovery has even been extended to couples who were engaged to be married.

However, a New Jersey case in 1980 did uphold these rights to a "wife" who was divorced after 23 years of marriage. As she and her "husband" reconciled after the divorce and planned to remarry, the court awarded her damages when an injury rendered the man impotent.

Although the California Court of Appeals upheld a cause of action for loss of consortium in a "stable and significant" live-in relationship in 1983, the same court denied recovery to another spousal equivalent in 1985. This opinion was upheld on appeal in 1988 on the basis of the California legislature's refusal to recognize a spousal equivalent as a party entitled to a recovery under the wrongful death statute in that state.

Legal commentators have advocated the elimination of the requirement of marriage in these claims. As the laws change and nonmarital cohabitation moves closer to recognition as a legal relationship, the requirement of a formal marriage may become less important.

Worker's Compensation

Although traditionally the courts have interpreted workers' compensation statutes to exclude unmarried cohabitants, several jurisdictions have awarded benefits to dependent cohabitants.

The objective of workers' compensation programs is to provide financial support to dependents of injured workers. The marital status of the dependents or moral judgments on a domestic situation have not been as important as the dependency of the claimant.

The award or denial of benefits is based on strict statutory construction of the laws of each state.

Any spousal equivalent who finds themselves in either of these two situations should investigate the possibility of receiving benefits. A landmark case in these areas is still to come.

Privileged communications

At common law, two doctrines exist regarding privileged communications between spouses. The first, sometimes described as the "anti-marital facts" privilege, disqualifies the adverse testimony of one spouse in an action against the other. The second is the privilege of marital communications, which bars testimony concerning confidential information exchanged between spouses.

The prevailing theory is that such a privilege does not exist between unmarried cohabitants. This is not surprising in view of the fact that courts have refused to extend this right when a marriage is either void, bigamous or a sham, i.e. a marriage for immigration purposes.

The Supreme Court modified the anti-marital privilege in 1980 so that a spouse who *wishes* to testify against the other may do so. The erosion of this privilege to married couples does not seem to indicate that an expansion of these rights to spousal equivalents will be forthcoming.

Changes

In 1989, the Denver City Council abolished an old zoning ordinance on the books that barred unmarried couples from living together in some of the city's classier neighborhoods. Meanwhile, in New York City, bereavement leave was granted to city workers whose "domestic partners" die.

New York's highest court attempted to re-define "family" in 1989 when it ruled that a man could remain in a rent-controlled apartment leased to his longtime companion. The trial court had ruled that the law prohibiting the landlord from evicting a family member of a deceased tenant did not apply to this spousal equivalent. The higher court was sympathetic enough to uphold "a means of protecting a certain class of occupants from the sudden loss of their homes," and contended that "a more realistic view of a family includes two adult lifetime partners whose relationship is long-term and characterized by an emotional and financial commitment and interdependence."

As was the case with *Marvin vs. Marvin,* California seems to be the leader in making changes. Santa Cruz allows city workers to sign an "Affidavit of Domestic Partnership" to qualify spousal equivalents for health benefits, signed under the penalty of perjury. West Hollywood allows those who "share the common necessities of life" to swear out a similar form which requires hospitals and jails to allow visitation. The city of Berkeley has extended health benefits to the unmarried partners of municipal employees since 1985.

San Francisco has the nation's strongest law of all which allows those who "share one another's lives in an intimate and committed relationship" to file a declaration making them eligible for status as "domestic partners." Unmarried couples, regardless of sex, must live together and be jointly responsible for basic living expenses. The declaration is registered with the county clerk for $35.00 and a termination notice may be filed if the relationship ends.

The ordinance also forbids discrimination by the city against such arrangements. City employees and their partners should now have the same rights to hospital visitation, sick leave, bereavement leave, and maternity leave as married employees. The mayor also appointed a task force to study the financial implications of extending health benefits to non-marital couples.

Stanford University in California opened their married student housing to unmarried couples in 1990, both opposite sex and same sex. The "domestic partners policy" requires students to establish that they are in a "long-term domestic partnership with a mutual commitment similar to that of marriage and share the necessities of life and responsibility for their common welfare."

The American Civil Liberties Union filed suit in Atlanta in 1990 against Continental Airlines on behalf of a gay couple who said they were discriminated against by the airline. Continental's frequent flier program refused to issue a companion ticket to one member of the couple under a two-for-one offer, claiming that only family members qualified. The couple, who have lived together for 32 years, were told they would have to produce a marriage license. (As members of this frequent flier program, the authors were pleased to find that the rules for companion tickets and transfer of frequent flier miles now read "anyone who lives at the same address.")

In March, 1991, Montefiore Medical Center, a hospital in the Bronx, became the largest private employer in the nation to provide health benefits for same sex couples who could prove their living arrangements were similar to married couples.

By adopting a concept of family more in line with the way people really live, these scattered instances have meant headway for all spousal equivalents.

What Can We Do?

More clearly defined boundaries need to be drawn to determine what constitutes a "family." Society benefits from long-term, supportive relationships. An alternative relationship that is happy and productive deserves some of its protections.

Spousal equivalents should continue to urge the creation of a system of legal rights that do not discriminate against their right to privacy and freedom of choice. This is particularly true of same sex couples as the law provides them no means to formalize their unions.

The denial of the right of same sex couples to enter into a marriage contract has been based on two arguments. The first is that the traditional and the legal definition of marriage is the "union of a man and a woman." The second is the fact that a primary incentive for marriage, historically, has been procreation and continuation of the species. Same sex couples don't fit the profile.

The denial of benefits to these couples, however, should not be based on semantics. A new legal term needs to be coined, and statutes allowing a legal relationship to be formed between same sex couples should be passed. These "domestic partners" could have licensing statutes and rules to follow for dissolution of a relationship similar to those governing marriage.

We need to remember that it was only in the 1960's that laws denying the right to marry between couples of different races were struck down. Similar discrimination exists as long as same sex couples are denied the right to legalize their relationships.

Not allowing people to determine their own definition of family, regardless of sexual preference, is a subtle form of prejudice. While there may be nothing to gain by flaunting a lack of marital status, there is no reason to be shy about your choice of an alternative lifestyle when it comes to standing up for your rights.

HOME, SWEET HOME

"I am a marvelous housekeeper. Every time I leave a man I keep his house."

Zsa Zsa Gabor

One of the most important decisions spousal equivalents make is where they are going to live.

Psychologically, it is often easier to establish a new home when the decision is made to move in together. A new apartment or house is a fresh start, and territorial arguments on one spousal equivalent's turf are eliminated. Obviously, this may not always be practical.

The following overview is designed to cover all the options of setting up housekeeping, and help you with the practical or legal ramifications before you make the move, or after. We will also discuss the theories of marital property ownership, which a well-informed spousal equivalent needs to know when weighing the options of continued cohabitation vs. marriage.

Renting Together

Be aware of the legal consequences of putting both of your names on a lease of a house or apartment. A joint lease does not mean that each spousal equivalent is liable for half the rent. It means that both have signed a contract which obligates each to pay the full amount of the rent and be totally responsible for any damages to the property if the other defaults.

An "understanding" of who pays the rent and who retains the residence in the event of a split may be fine, but a cohabitation agreement is better.

Moving into your Spousal Equivalent's Home

This option requires both sensitivity and tact, for creating "our" home out of "your" home can be a delicate matter. Don't let the practical aspects overwhelm the situation.

If the residence you decide to live in is a rental, it is wise to review the lease agreement to determine if there are any restrictions which would be violated by this new arrangement. Also, it is possible that, under certain circumstances, the spousal equivalent moving in is committing to obligations not specifically set out in the lease.

Any oral agreement with the landlord regarding the new arrangement might well be binding, and paying rent directly to a landlord or management company could give rise to an implied contract which creates a landlord–tenant obligation.

This is Pat and Mike's situation. The lease on their apartment is in Pat's name, but the landlord knows Mike lives there. Mike often pays the rent from his checking account. Unknowingly, he could be placing himself in a position where he is fully responsible for the rent if Pat moved out.

If one spousal equivalent owns property already, this potential problem and any other landlord headaches are eliminated. But what if one of you is going to pay a portion of the mortgage as rent? Does this give you any rights to the property? Read on, and the ins and outs of owning a shared home will be explained.

Buying Together

Some communities and neighborhoods have zoning ordinances prohibiting unrelated people from living together. The United States Supreme Court upheld the constitutionality of such a law in 1974. These housing laws have been used to harass both same sex and opposite sex couples. Before you buy, or before you merge your households, make sure this isn't a problem. To counteract this discrimination, some states have prohibited local communities from enacting housing laws discriminating against unrelated people.

Homeownership has many advantages. It signifies stability, eliminates landlords, and offers tax advantages and a hedge against inflation. If you are buying a home together, it can be both a spiritual and economic venture. Make the experience a pleasant one by knowing the basics of home ownership.

When contemplating the purchase of a home, one of the first things to consider is whose name to put on the deed. Homes can be owned in one of three ways in most states:

⌂   one person holds title;

⌂   both of you hold title as "joint tenants;

⌂   both of you hold title as "tenants in
common."

One Spousal Equivalent on the Deed

If you are moving into or living in a home which is
deeded in only one name, there is no problem if the
spousal equivalent owner is paying all the household
expenses. In the real world, though, that is rarely the
case.

Whatever decisions you have made about sharing
expenses, it is likely that the non-owner spousal
equivalent is paying either rent or a share of living
expenses to offset the mortgage. And what about the
new carpet for the bedroom that you buy together, or
the new wallpaper in the dining room?

The non-owner spousal equivalent is obviously in
need of compensation for any expenses which help the
owner spousal equivalent build equity in the solely
owned property. Insist on a cohabitation agreement.
As well as building equity, the owner spousal
equivalent is receiving the benefits of the tax write-off
of home ownership. Don't forget these factors when
determining a fair division of monthly shared expenses.

Nick and Nora have made a fairly equitable
arrangement, for Nick pays all expenses relating to his
house and Nora does not pay Nick any specific rent.
Her contribution to the utilities, however, saves him
money monthly, and helps them both feel as if Nora is
pulling her weight. Nora also makes occasional
improvements, such as curtains, paint, or wallpaper,
but her expense is not so great that she feels Nick
would be obligated to reimburse her if she moved out.

Joint Tenancy

This form of property ownership means that you take title to real property and share the ownership 50/50, retaining the right to use the entire property. Additionally, if one joint tenant dies, the other can take the deceased's share if "right of survivorship" requirements are satisfied, even if there is a will leaving the property to someone else.

Each joint tenant also retains the right to sell their interest, regardless of the wishes of the other. This sale, however, would end the joint tenancy and create a tenancy in common with the new owner.

The creation of a joint tenancy depends on the language on the deed. Spousal equivalents can be joint tenants of the house they live in as well as any other real property.

Tenants in Common

The basic difference between joint tenants and tenants in common is that there is no right of survivorship. Upon the death of one owner, title is left to the beneficiaries in a will or the persons inheriting through the intestate (dying without a will) succession laws established in the state where the property is located. Tenants in common can own property in unequal shares as well, unlike joint tenants.

Property originally bought as tenants in common can be changed to joint tenancy by recording a new deed specifying the change. Spousal equivalents must determine the advantages and disadvantages of each form of property ownership on the facts of their individual situation.

Separate or Community?

Most couples who marry are unaware of the complexities and the subtleties of the property rights which come with a marriage license. For spousal equivalents who contemplate marriage in the future, it is important to know the laws in your home state. These laws apply both to real estate and personal possessions.

The fifty states are divided into separate property and community property states. Each state has attached its own interpretations to the property theory it has adopted, making generalizations difficult. The definitions that follow are basic ones only.

A total of 42 states and the District of Columbia apply the English common law theory of *separate property* to marital property ownership. The basic idea behind this theory is that all property and income acquired before or during the marriage belongs to the acquiring spouse.

As a result, a wife who was a homemaker could find herself destitute if her husband left her and all the property was in his name. In defense of this theory, divorce was seldom an issue as the system developed. When divorce became widespread, alimony became the equitable response to separate property ownership.

The idea of marital *community property* arose from the Napoleonic Code. The premise of community property is that everything accumulated during a marriage from the labor of either spouse belongs equally to both. The opposite side of this coin is that the debts and obligations are divided the same way.

Most of the states that use this system were strongly influenced by Spanish and French law.

Community property states include Arizona, California, Idaho, Louisiana, New Mexico, Nevada, Texas, Washington and Wisconsin. Of the community property states, only Texas courts are prohibited from also awarding alimony.

Each spouse may own property in a community property state that is classified as separate property if it is brought into the marriage or acquired through gift or inheritance while married.

Cohabitation Agreements and your Home

Housing is usually the most expensive item in any spousal equivalent's budget. Besides the financial aspects, a home is a very emotional possession for most of us. If you buy a home together, it is often the biggest asset that spousal equivalents share.

A cohabitation agreement between two joint tenants or two tenants in common should spell out who will remain on the property in the event of a separation, as well as a basis for compensation for the party who moves out.

Mutual obligations of sharing a residence should not be left to chance. A written agreement is the only guarantee that offers protection to the spousal equivalent, no matter what the choice of residence.

TO POOL OR NOT TO POOL?   8

When you are in love with someone you want to be near him all the time, except when you are out buying things and charging them to him.

Miss Piggy

Miss Piggy may be every man's nightmare, but she certainly illustrates the importance of reaching an agreement on the financial issues of living together.

Most of us have had to deal with renting an apartment, opening a bank account, paying monthly bills and, in short, doing all the things that it takes to live day-to-day in our modern world. When you make the decision to share your life with someone, dealing with these everyday issues suddenly changes.

Do you keep separate bank accounts or do you put all the money in one account? Do you split up the monthly expenses and each pay a portion or do you pay bills out of a joint account? Should you be able to sign on the other's bank account? Did one of you bring assets to the relationship that the other uses, such as a car or a home? Does one of you contribute to the maintenance of another's assets, such as overseeing rental property?

The fact that a joint responsibility between spousal equivalents has been created can cut your problems in half, or multiply them tenfold, depending on how you handle the practical financial matters facing the two of you as a couple.

Should you Pool your Money?

It is not recommended that spousal equivalents pool their joint financial resources. In these liberated times, it is not uncommon for married couples to have "his" money and "her" money, so spousal equivalents seem to have little incentive to deposit their paychecks and earnings into the same account.

Maintaining separate bank accounts, savings and investments is not only wise, but often essential for tax purposes. And commingling of funds can make a liaison dangerous, or at least inconvenient, for either party in the event of separation, death or disability.

The Joint Household Account

Pat and Mike still get money from their parents each month for living expenses. Mike's parents are in a significantly better financial position than Nora, and they were pretty generous with Mike while he was in undergraduate school. But, since he began work on his master's degree and his younger brother started college last fall, his money situation has tightened up.

Pat works fifteen hours a week as a secretary in the business school at the university, and Mike has a night watchman job at a private dorm on Friday and Saturday nights. Pat brings home about $400.00 per month, and Mike brings home about $350.00. Their rent is only $150.00 a month because of their work with the management company. They opened a joint household account and each of them deposits 60% of their paycheck into the account on payday, with the idea that a percentage is fairer than a set amount.

So far, there has been enough in the account each month to cover the rent, phone, electricity, and food. Each has money from their parents and some left over from their checks for personal expenses such as clothes, long distance, etc.

Pat and Mike plan to marry once he has finished his graduate work. Like many college couples, they want to keep their options open and keep the money coming from home. Marrying at this stage in their lives might mean parental problems that neither wants. At this point in their relationship, the financial risks are minor. They have little property to argue over, and the payoffs of their education are yet to come.

Pat and Mike don't worry as much about who pays for what as they do about whether they can pay for something, period. Pat paid Mike's car insurance last month when he was overdrawn at the bank. Mike paid for Pat's doctor bills a few months back when she had a bad case of the flu and couldn't work. They don't keep a running total of who pays for what other than the contribution to the account, and are both willing to help the other when they can.

Sharing Expenses

A 50–50 split of expenses between two spousal equivalents who bring home a equivalent income would be a simple solution to the issue of sharing expenses. However, the inequity in earning power between men and women means that rarely is such an equal division of expenses fair to both sides in any real life situation. An agreement to contribute proportionately based on income makes sense, but may tend to create resentment on the part of the person carrying the

bigger load or mean a loss of independence on the one
with the lighter. Here's how our three other couples
manage.

William and Mary

William and Mary keep separate accounts, and
decided against opening a joint account. Mary already
has a business account and a personal account, and
didn't want the headaches of a third account. William
has numerous accounts of his own, and agreed that
another account was just one more checkbook to keep
up with and another service charge to pay.

Instead, William pays the mortgage each month,
and Mary pays all the other household expenses.
Because Mary has cash flow problems in her business
and cannot effectively estimate her profit for any given
month and because she handles the running of the
household, William agreed to pay 60% of their joint
total outlay each month.

On the last day of each month, Mary gives William
a list of bills she has paid. To balance out the
mortgage payment, she handles most monthly
expenses out of her personal account. She pays all the
utilities, the lawn maintenance, the maid, the
groceries, and other miscellaneous expenses. Over a
six month period of using this system, they found they
were within approximately one hundred dollars of each
other in money spent on living expenses.

Nick and Nora

Nick and Nora are very careful about keeping their
finances separate. All of their checking accounts and

other financial arrangements are in their individual names only.

Nora pays for the household cleaning supplies, toiletries for them both, and the groceries. Nick pays the insurance and taxes on his house, electricity, gas, water, and the telephone, all of which are in his name. They share entertainment and travel costs.

Nick's the type of person who is a big tipper and Nora figures lunch checks with her friends to the penny. But they accept this about each other, and work around it. If Nick knows that Nora wants something special, but she is trying to economize so that she can send extra money to Pat, he'll surprise her with a new purse, or a hardcover book when he knows she'll wait on the paperback. He figures she's saving him money by clipping coupons and checking for the best values at the grocery store, and she knows he's probably right, and loves being spoiled with the occasional present.

Bob and Ted

Of the four couples, Bob and Ted probably have the most complicated financial situation. Bob makes what he refers to as an "obscene" amount of money, and Ted has his occasional monetary successes when he sells a painting. Bob pays all the necessary living expenses, and Ted repays him by renovating his rental property.

Both Bob and Ted have been in relationships in the past that cost them financially. Bob opened joint credit card accounts with a former lover, and found himself paying for the entire amounts when the man skipped town. Ted had a car that he loaned to a former boyfriend who agreed to pay for the insurance, and he only found out that the policy had lapsed when the car was totalled.

Bob and Ted are lucky in that both of them are very generous people.   The last time Ted sold a painting, he treated the two of them to a ski week in Canada.   They consider themselves to be fully committed to one another and, because there is plenty of money to support their lifestyle, do not worry unduly about who pays for what. Bob's financial planner and his CPA encourage him to formalize a business relationship with Ted, and they both agree this is a good idea in principle, but haven't had the time to get around to it.

Different financial styles can be one of the biggest problems facing any couple, so learn to recognize that opposites attract and proper planning eliminates future financial problems.

"Bachelors should be heavily taxed. It is not fair that some men should be happier than others."

Oscar Wilde

Up to now, we have been discussing the social and legal implications of being a spousal equivalent, and the day-to-day considerations involving such necessary matters as budgeting finances, sharing expenses, purchasing property together and the like. Addressing these issues early on in the relationship and reducing these decisions to writing will avoid misunderstandings.

The next issue to be confronted when considering the structure of your joint financial venture is how to take maximum advantage of the federal and state tax laws.

Income Taxes

Complying with federal and state income tax requirements may be one of the major legal problems that you and your partner will confront. At first glance, this may seem simple. You get the forms in the mail each January, fill them out by reporting your income and deductions, sign the form and mail it back. No problem, right?

Well, perhaps. We wish it were that simple. In your specific situation, it may well be. But for many spousal equivalents, there are questions of how jointly earned income is to be reported, who gets the deductions; indeed, what kind of return needs to be filed.

First things first – what about filing status? The Congress passes the laws which the Internal Revenue Service administers. These laws are embodied in the Internal Revenue Code (IRC). To date, Congress does not allow unmarried couples to file a joint return. The cohabitating couple has no joint filing rights. Each person is responsible for filing his or her own tax return, if one is required.

Occasionally, the question comes up about one party claiming the other as a dependent. We think there are several problems with this and do not recommend it. However, since every situation is different, you should consult a qualified tax consultant in your state.

In most situations, the IRS will follow the applicable state law relating to the particular situation. For example, the IRS recognizes the community property laws of those states which are community property states. Tax returns from those states must follow community property concepts. Likewise, a dependency relationship will not be upheld if it violates local law (even if all other dependency tests are met).

Bob and Ted

In order to illustrate some common tax problems, consider Bob and Ted's situation. Last year, Bob and Ted had a combined income of $200,000. Bob earned

$195,000 as a surgeon and Ted received a $5,000 commission to produce a series of paintings for a local upscale restaurant.

Bob is purchasing the home in which they live. There is a current mortgage on the home which Bob pays monthly, and he also owns rental property. Ted collects the rents, maintains the property and, in general, oversees all management activities in connection with the properties. Bob pays all of the living expenses and gives Ted money occasionally. Ted does the cooking, cleaning and shopping. Neither party infers that sexual services are part of their arrangement.

For 1990, Bob prepares his income tax return and reports income of $195,000 less deductions for interest and taxes applicable to his residence. He also reports the rental income from the rent property and the deductions applicable thereto. Ted owes no income tax on the $5,000 he earned.

Is this scenario familiar? The situation appears to be fairly simple; a high earner supporting a low earner, the high earner paying the bills, the low earner providing services and expertise for the common good. The high earner files a tax return, the low earner does not. But wait—doesn't Ted have earnings he is not considering? And does Bob have an additional deduction he is not taking?

The point of tax law established here is that Bob and Ted have entered into a contract, albeit verbally, where Ted performs bona fide services for Bob in exchange for support. Under the IRC, such services represent compensation to Ted. To the extent these services are for the rental property, Bob may be entitled to a deduction. But where the services are personal in nature, i.e., cooking, cleaning, shopping, etc. no deduction is allowed. Remember that the IRC does not recognize a personal relationship between Bob and Ted but may ascribe a business relationship to them.

In *Whorton vs. Dillingham*, a California decision involving a same sex couple, the court noted that adults who live together and engage in sexual relations are competent to contract regarding their earnings and property rights. Quoting *Marvin*, the court also said, "Such contracts will be enforced unless expressly and inseparably based upon an illicit consideration of sexual services."

As noted elsewhere in the text, not all states follow the California lead. Look at Appendix A for the law in your state and consult with your attorney for the current judicial rulings in this area if you need further information.

William and Mary

Let's continue our examples by considering William and Mary's situation. William and Mary share all living expenses.   This situation is fairly common among spousal equivalents.   Most usually work and share expenses.   William and Mary each file his or her own tax return reporting their respective earnings and deductions. Again, this seems fairly straightforward. But the IRS has managed to lay a few traps for the unwary.

First, the IRS will not allow a person to take a deduction where he is paying an expense on property which is owned by someone else. For example, one spousal equivalent cannot take a deduction for a share of mortgage interest or taxes on property the other spousal equivalent owns even though they have agreed to split these expenses 50-50, or in some other proportion. Only the one who owns the property can take the deduction. Contrast this treatment with the married couple.

Second, even though the incomes are substantially equal and there is a written agreement with regard to sharing expenses, the IRS could assert that rental income should be imputed to the owner-spousal equivalent, i.e. because Mary pays all household expenses, she is effectively paying rental income to William.

What can you do? First, recognize that you and your spousal equivalent do not enjoy the same rights under the IRC as married filing jointly do. You are, in the eyes of the IRS, two single individuals who happen to share the same address. As such, the agreements that you have reached with respect to taking care of day-to-day business should certainly be in writing. Perhaps one of you will pay the mortgage while the other pays for food, supplies, utilities, etc. At the end of the month, give the other a full accounting of the month's expenses.

While there is no guarantee that an IRS examination won't delve into personal living arrangements, neither is there the likelihood that an agent would propose capricious, unfounded adjustments. The best safeguard to this sort of examination is documentation and consistency of action. Decide how you want to structure your financial life, put it in writing and stick to it.

Continued Cohabitation vs. Marriage

Your income tax is calculated according to the bracket you are in. Beginning in 1991, the IRC provides for 3 brackets. The lowest is 15%, the middle is 28% and the highest is 31%. As your income increases, you will move into a higher bracket. The point where the higher rate applies is different for married and single taxpayers. This is also a point where proper tax planning is important, particularly if you are contemplating a change in your marital status.

Generally, married persons file a joint return. Both spouses report their income on the same return which may result in a portion of their combined incomes being taxed at a higher rate than would be the case if they could file as single individuals. While not the classic definition, this is certainly a form of "bracket creep."

In addition, marrieds are only allowed to either itemize deductions *or* take a standard deduction. Spousal equivalents, since they are taxed as single individuals, have more flexibility. For example, one could itemize so as to deduct home mortgage interest and property taxes along with charitable contributions, tax and financial planning fees, some legal fees and unreimbursed employee business expenses to name a few. The other could take the standard deduction.

Since each situation is different, it is always best to consult your tax adviser.

If you are contemplating marriage (or divorce), the timing may be important so as to maximize tax advantages. If you are married on December 31, the IRS considers you to have been married the entire year.

Again, consult a knowledgeable adviser. It could mean significant savings for you.

Delinquent Taxes and the Spousal Equivalent

Spousal equivalents need to be aware of problems which can arise when one party owes delinquent taxes to the IRS. The IRS has the power to file a lien to attach an individual's salary when delinquent taxes are owed. Currently, in Texas, the IRS takes the position that one-half of a new spouse's salary can also be attached to satisfy the tax delinquency, following the community property theory that one-half of the salary earned by a spouse is the community property of the other.

The IRS will extend this argument to a common-law marriage as well. Fortunately, a cohabitation agreement can be used to defeat this particular allegation since it clearly states that the parties have not entered into a marriage. As with other financial matters, it is necessary that spousal equivalents be straightforward about any potential tax problems before the cohabitation agreement is executed.

PERSONAL
FINANCIAL PLANNING _____10

"Why is there so much month left at the end of the money?"
Unknown

Personal financial planning is not just for spousal equivalents; indeed, it is for everyone. Financial planning is an ongoing systematic approach to planning for your financial needs at some future time. It is a continuing process of maximizing available financial resources. This future time may be retirement, but it also might be education for your children, care of an elderly parent or protection against some major calamity. As an organized discipline, financial planning has only recently appeared on the scene, but the component parts have long been a part of our financial lives.

In the past forty years, Americans have attained a level of affluence and standard of living never before accomplished. But with this status has come problems: inflation, huge levels of personal and government debt, the near collapse of the social security system and the actual collapse of many banks and savings and loan institutions.

These problems do not have simple solutions but, as the baby boomers look ahead to their retirement years, it is clear that personal savings programs need to be implemented so as to make the "golden years" comfortable. The baby boomers are beginning to feel the triple squeeze, i.e., education for their children, support of their parents and retirement savings for themselves.

Rare indeed is the individual who stays with the same employer for forty years. Most of us change jobs every seven to ten years. It is not likely that an employer funded retirement plan will meet our retirement needs. We have also programmed ourselves to doubt that we will see any benefit from the thousands of dollars we annually pump into the social security coffers.

Even so, because Americans are not savers, we must rely, in part, on company pension plans and social security to provide for our needs after retirement. However, studies tell us repeatedly that this will not be enough. It is estimated that only one out of 100 retirees is completely self supporting. The rest depend, in varying degrees, on family, friends or government.

Set Goals And Objectives

A well developed financial plan can enable you to realize your financial goals and objectives in a deliberate, organized manner. In order to help you meet your goals and objectives, the first step is to carefully define what those goals and objectives are.

If you can clearly state your goals, you have accomplished several things. First, you have had to carefully consider exactly what those goals are. Second, you have had to prioritize these goals in some manner. Third, you have probably prioritized achievable goals taking into account your present and foreseeable circumstances.

Once you have completed this analysis, you are in position to implement the steps necessary to accomplish the overall goals. A financial plan that makes sense for you can be developed after a thorough analysis of your current available resources and the resources you are likely to generate in the future.

A financial planner will want to find out as much as he can about you. It is his job to present those options to you which will best help you achieve your objectives. Depending on your current resources and future needs, he may present recommendations utilizing different types of insurance or investment programs which can accomplish these objectives.

William and Mary

Remember William and Mary? He is 38 and salaried. She is 35 and owns her own business. At a cocktail party recently, they met a financial planner who invited them to come by her office for a consultation. She asked them to carefully consider their individual goals and objectives before the consultation to make the meeting more productive.

William feels that his most important goal is to provide a college education for his five year old son. Also, he would like to provide himself with a retirement income of $36,000 annually at age 65.

Mary would like to work at building her business for another 20 years and then retire with a annual retirement income of $35,000. She believes she could sell her business at retirement for approximately $400,000 after taxes in today's dollars. However, she worries that the business is too dependent on her. Its value would be wiped out if she were to become seriously ill or disabled for an extended period of time.

Both William and Mary believe that inflation will continue at about 4% per year, but that they can realize an after tax return of 7% on their investments. Neither is counting on social security or company pension plans.

William further estimates that it would take $7,000 per year in today's dollars to provide his son with a college education beginning in 13 years. Based on this information, the financial planner quantifies the goals as follows:

Cost of education–years 13–16 with inflation at 4% per year	$ 49,496
	=========
After tax dollars needed now to provide for education years 13–16	$ 20,539
	=========

If William were financially able to invest $20,539 now at a return of 7% after taxes, he would have an education fund of $49,496 in year 13 when his son begins college. Alternatively, the financial planner shows William that he may invest $2,458 annually for 13 years which would accomplish the same goal. Thus, in this way, William is able to systematically fund his primary goal: his son's college education.

William also wants to start saving now toward his eventual retirement in 27 years. At that time, he wants a nest egg which will allow him to withdraw the then equivalent of $36,000 per year over his remaining life expectancy. According to actuarial tables, the life expectancy for a male at age 65 is 15 years. The financial planner quantifies William's goal as follows:

Annual income needs
during retirement $ 36,000
                                          ==========

Inflation adjustment:
27 years at 4%   2.883
                                          ==========

Equivalent income needs
future dollars year 27 $ 103,788
                                          ==========

Accumulation needed at
retirement with 7% after
tax return subject to
4% inflation $1,285,459
                                          ==========

This calculation tells us that William will need to accumulate $1,285,459 at retirement in 27 years in order to draw out the then equivalent of $36,000 per year over his remaining life expectancy.

With inflation at 4% per year, this means that $36,000 today will be worth only $34,560 in equivalent purchasing power one year from today. William has to increase his withdrawals to $37,440 to maintain the same purchasing power that he has today. With inflation at 4% per year, he will have to increase his withdrawals by 4% each year. Extend this concept 27 years into the future and one can readily see the eroding effect of grinding inflation. Fortunately, William expects to earn 7% after taxes to offset the effects of inflation and to help him accumulate the needed funds.

The question now is how does William go about accumulating these funds? Since the $1,285,459 represents an inflation adjusted amount and considering that he has 27 years in which to accumulate this amount, the financial planner has to deflate this to current dollars.

Retirement fund needed	$1,285,459
	==========
Deflation adjustment:	
27 years at 4%	.3468
	==========
Present value of fund today	$ 445,797
	==========
Annual savings required–Year 1	$ 11,133
	==========

William needs to save annually $11,133 (adjusted annually for inflation, of course) to reach his goal at the end of year 27. For those interested in the math steps required for these calculations, see Appendix B.

Mary believes that she will be able to pocket $400,000 in today's dollars at age 55 from the sale of her business. She intends to retire at that time and would like to have an income of $35,000 per year in today's dollars. Unlike William, she does not want to diminish her beginning principal. In order to see if her goals are realistic, the financial planner makes the following calculations:

Principal sum needed at retirement to provide an income of $35,000 per year with inflation at 4% per year	$ 1,095,562

Future value of $400,000 20 years at 4% inflation	$ 876,449

Subtracting–Mary will be short of her needed accumulation by	$ 219,113

===========

Assuming Mary's assumptions about inflation and her after-tax return from the sale of her business are correct, she will be short of the accumulation she needs for retirement at her stated support level of $35,000 (in today's dollars). She either needs to reassess her goals or make additional investments over the next 20 years which will enable her to retire with the annual income she requires.

The financial planner recommends to Mary that she start an IRA savings program now. She can put $2,000 per year in an IRA now, get a tax write-off and accumulate earnings which will remain tax-free until she withdraws them. Mary believes she can earn 10% per year in an IRA since the earnings are not subject to taxation currently. After further computation, the financial planner advises Mary that the IRA will yield an additional accumulation of $126,005 in 20 years leaving Mary $93,108 short of her goal.

After further consideration, Mary decides to accept the plan for now but wants to review it again soon to see if the shortfall can be made up when the company is more profitable. The planner points out that Mary can switch to a self-employed retirement plan, where she can save more than $2,000 per year, when she can afford it. (For those readers curious about the shortfall Mary experienced, she could overcome this with additional before tax savings of $1,478 per year.)

Since Mary is also concerned about the continuance of the business and her income in the event of serious illness or disability, the financial planner recommends that she consider purchasing disability insurance. This would provide Mary with a monthly income as well as owner's business continuation funds if she became incapacitated. Mary also plans to involve a trusted associate in more of the business decisions and operating needs.

As Mary and William leave the meeting, both feel very positive about their plans now that they have quantified their primary goals and have taken steps to implement those goals.

"For the memory of men slips and flows away, and the life of man is short, and that which is not written is soon forgotten."

Beaumanoir, French legal scholar, in the year 1283

The odds are stacked against an unmarried couple. The death or incapacity of a partner or the end of a relationship can be emotionally devastating. Why risk potential financial devastation as well?

It has been estimated that nearly two-thirds of all adults do not have adequate wills. Over 95% have failed to prepare other estate planning instruments such as trusts, powers of attorney, or living wills. You don't have to be rich to be a candidate for estate planning.

Last Will and Testaments

A simple will guarantees that you have control over who gets your assets. Attorneys don't make money drawing up wills—they make money probating estates for the people who didn't.

Regardless of how you wish to provide for your spousal equivalent, picture your family arguing over what belonged to you and what belonged to your live-in. Spare everyone the trauma.

A will is, simply, a document which specifies who receives your property when you die. It's easy to make and gives you the opportunity to leave your property to the people of your choice, not the people designated by statute if you die without one. Also, a will can be easily revoked if you change your mind about any bequests you might have made.

Nick had his will reviewed when he and Nora moved in together. Nora did not have a will, and she decided this was a good time to make these decisions.

Like many older couples, Nick and Nora do not want to create problems for their children because of their new living arrangement. Because Texas is a community property state, Nick's late wife left her 50% of their estate to him with the understanding that he would leave his estate to their children. But, at the same time, Nick does not want Nora to be homeless if something happened to him.

Nora's only significant asset is her alimony, which will terminate when she dies. The few possessions she does have will go to her children, including the antiques she inherited from her mother. Because these possessions are in Nick's house, she doesn't want there to be a problem if something happened to her.

Nick and Nora consulted an attorney regarding these issues. He told them that a will can catalyze all the elements of an estate and tie all loose ends together. He pointed out that everyone needs a will because, no matter how small a piece of the pie there may be, that doesn't mean your survivors won't argue over it.

Anyone who has attained adult status in their home state and who is of sound mind can make a will. In most states, unless a spousal equivalent is still legally married or has children, there is nothing to prevent bequests to the person with whom you live.

The differences in state laws make it imperative that you contact an attorney to prepare your will. The statutes vary from state to state, so using a standard form can be dangerous. A simple will, without elaborate bequests, can be prepared for a minimum amount of money. Refer to Chapter Thirteen and the information on hiring an attorney for suggestions on finding an attorney who can keep costs reasonable.

Hand-written ("holographic") wills are valid in many states, but are not recommended. They are looked upon with suspicion by the courts, and rightly so. A hand-written will is a risky business.

Joint wills should also be avoided. This type of will attempts to dictate to the survivor how the deceased's property will be distributed upon the survivor's death. Obviously, once someone has inherited your property, it would be impossible to enforce what they do with it. It seems useless to try.

It is a good idea to have an existing will reviewed if you move to a new state. Also, depending on state laws, your will may need to be changed:

O when you marry;

O when you divorce;

O when children are born or adopted;

O when you accumulate significant property;

O when federal legislation may affect your will.

In many states, marrying or divorcing can actually nullify an existing will.

Another aspect of distribution of property which is often overlooked is the care of pets. Unfortunately, it is foreseeable that pets could be euthanized after an owner's death, no matter what the marital status of the owner. It is possible no one, not even your spousal equivalent, would be willing to accept the responsibility of caring for your pets. Make sure you include pets in your will to avoid this situation, and inform the person you select as their caretaker that you have done so.

A promise to take on such a responsibility can be relied on much more than the vague hope that friends or family would cherish your pets as much as you do. (As a footnote, joint pets should probably be included in a cohabitation agreement as well. Consider the best interest of the pet when making provisions for their care in the event of dissolution of your relationship.)

Once you have stopped procrastinating and executed your last will and testament, store your will in a safe place. Putting the will in a safety deposit box is a potential problem, or at least an inconvenience, unless your executors have access to it.

A will can be revoked in the following ways:

○ execution of a new will with revocation language;

○ destroying the will itself, preferably in front of witnesses, to eliminate the possibility of testimony that the will is merely missing.

Insurance

The distribution of proceeds from life insurance policies are not determined by a will. When an individual purchases a life insurance policy, he has entered into a contract with his insurance company. His will does not override this contract.

When one purchases an insurance policy, he has the same rights of ownership as he would have with any other asset. He has the obligation to pay the premiums when due but also the right to name the beneficiary. In fact, he can have the death proceeds paid to one or several beneficiaries upon his demise. He can also name his own estate to be beneficiary, thus, providing liquidity to pay any death, (i.e. inheritance), taxes. Please note that the insurance proceeds are exempt from **income** taxes but, if the estate is large enough, may be subject to **inheritance** taxes.

If inheritance taxes are a concern, an insurance trust may be the answer to avoid this problem. One could set up an irrevocable trust, fund it with an annual contribution of cash, and have the trust own insurance policies–the premiums of which are paid for by the cash gifts. (For comments on gifts and trusts, refer to the next section on Estate Planning.) The downside to this planning technique is that the individual has permanently shifted to the trust one of his most important rights–the ability to change his beneficiary. Still, insurance trusts for large estates are an important estate planning tool.

Life insurance generally falls into two categories. The first type is "term" insurance, where the premiums pay only for a death benefit feature. Term insurance typically has no cash or loan values. This insurance is usually inexpensive in one's early years but the premiums increase as one ages. At death, the insurance proceeds are includable in the decedent's estate.

This is the type of insurance that William and Mary have. William had two insurance policies when he met Mary. After they moved in together, he made her the beneficiary of one of the policies, with his son the alternate as well as beneficiary of the other policy. Mary purchased a new policy and made William the beneficiary. This way, both are assured of being able to pay the mortgage on the townhouse and not suffer financial loss along with the emotional loss of losing a partner.

The second type of insurance is called by many names but has one distinguishing characteristic—it has a cash value feature. As you pay premiums, some portion of the premium dollar provides pure insurance protection (as in the term policy) and some portion is set aside for a savings feature (as if you put the cash into a bank account).

Bob has this kind of policy. The premiums remain level and do not increase with age. Ted doesn't have insurance at all, but Bob would suffer no economic loss if something happened to Ted. As the more practical of the two, however, he has made sure that Ted is well provided for through his insurance policies.

As with the term insurance, the proceeds are includable in the decedent's estate. Of course, the insurance industry has seen to it that there are many permutations to these basic features; your insurance agent will be happy to explain the lines of coverage he offers to best suit your needs.

One other point about life insurance is worth noting. You may consider "cross-insuring" (where you would own a policy on your spousal equivalent's life). After all, married couples do this often (or business partners). But, unfortunately, this is not possible. The insurance industry requires an "insurable interest" before a policy can be issued. To date, they do not recognize your relationship with your spousal equivalent in the same light that they recognize marrieds or business partners. Hopefully, as the demand becomes greater, they will alter their stance.

Estate Planning

Proper estate planning is a must for everyone, married or not. Generally, if the net value of an estate is more than $600,000 at the time of death, it will be taxable. Because of the marital deduction, married couples may have nontaxable estates up to $1.2 million. Spousal equivalents do not have the marital deduction option available to them, which makes estate planning even more important for those with significant assets.

There is no doubt that $600,000 is a sizeable estate, but with proceeds from the three largest assets of the typical estate (insurance, home, and business interests), the $600,000 threshold could easily be exceeded, even if you don't feel that wealthy. Personal items such as furniture, jewelry, and autos are taxed at their fair market values, as are investments such as stocks, bonds, or land.

The Internal Revenue Code permits a donor to give up to $10,000 each year per donee with no gift tax consequences. The $10,000 can be in money or in property. If in property, it is the market value of the property on the date of the gift. This is an excellent tool to reduce one's estate. Since the future earnings and/or appreciation of the gift are also removed from one's estate, this has a double barrelled effect.

The IRS requires that a gift tax return be filed on gifts exceeding $10,000. It is wise to file a return if property is given even if less than $10,000 so as to remove any future question as to fair market value at the time of the gift. Filing a return also begins the period for the statute of limitations, which is in the donor's favor in dealings with the IRS.

Trusts

Living and Testamentary Trusts

The trust is one of the most important tools to proper estate planning. With it, you can reduce or eliminate income taxes and estate taxes, avoid probate and protect your heirs. When you give property in trust, you are allowing someone else to manage your property for the benefit of yourself or your beneficiaries.

Trusts are of two basic types: testamentary and living (sometimes called inter-vivos). Testamentary trusts are created by your will and take effect after death. A testamentary trust would not have tax advantages, but would allow you to use assets for the benefit of one person during their lifetime, with the remaining principal to be left to another after the beneficiary's death.

In fact, this is what Bob has done to protect Ted, in addition to the insurance policy. He does not want Ted to have all of his assets, as he feels he is naive about money matters. But he wants him to have the income from his assets to maintain his lifestyle.   He feels a testamentary trust accomplishes this goal.

Living trusts, as the term implies, are created during your lifetime but may continue after death. The main advantage of a living trust is that they can be used to avoid probate.   However, setting up and maintaining the trust can be an expensive proposition. This form of estate planning is only recommended for those spousal equivalents who have significant assets.

There are two kinds of living trusts–revocable or irrevocable.

Revocable Trusts

A trust is revocable if you, as grantor, can alter or revoke the terms, conditions or beneficiaries of the trust.   There is no income tax benefit to this type of trust.   But there are other advantages.

The property placed in the revocable trust can be managed by a trustee and the income paid to you during your life. At your death, the principal of the trust is paid to your beneficiaries.   The assets of the trust are not subject to probate.

Since probated estates are subject to public scrutiny, this allows you to retain privacy over your assets.   The assets will, however, be included in your estate for inheritance tax purposes since you retained the right during your life to revoke or alter the terms and beneficiaries of the trust.

Irrevocable Trusts

An irrevocable trust is just that—once set up, you cannot revoke it or alter its terms. In this type of trust, you do not pay the tax on the trust income. That burden is passed to the trust itself or to its beneficiaries if the income is distributed. The property placed in the trust is also removed from your estate, although there may be gift tax consequences depending on the value of the property.

If you think that you would like to know more about the use of trusts in your estate planning, discuss the subject with your accountant or attorney. Trusts are an excellent way to provide for your spousal equivalent while saving on taxes and retaining privacy.

Powers of Attorney

Durable Powers of Attorney

A power of attorney is a legal document which authorizes one person to act in another's behalf. The person making the power of attorney is called the principal. The person given the power of attorney is called the attorney-in-fact.

In the event of an emergency, it is imperative that someone has the ability to handle financial and practical matters of the person stricken. A court proceeding, known as a guardianship, custodianship, or conservatorship, depending on the jurisdiction, can determine who has that right, but these proceedings are expensive and time consuming. Planning ahead with a power of attorney can avoid this complicated situation.

Nick's attorney advised him that a general power of attorney does not survive the incapacity of the principal, and would not prevent the intervention of the courts. Only a durable power of attorney can accomplish this, as it specifically allows an attorney-in-fact to continue to make decisions when the principal cannot.

Durable powers of attorney have different requirements in different states. Regardless of where they are drafted, however, the flexibility of such documents makes them indispensable for spousal equivalents.

Medical Powers of Attorney

You may be closer to your spousal equivalent than anyone else. If one of you becomes ill or disabled, however, neither of you have a legal right to make decisions regarding medical treatment for each other.

A medical power of attorney will prevent this from happening. This idea arose in the gay community when lifelong partners were denied a say in medical treatment and often found that their hospital visits could be limited.

Critical issues such as choice of hospital or treating doctors, methods of treatment, and use of life support equipment, arise with a serious illness. Bob and Ted have both executed medical powers of attorney for each other. They have seen too many situations where frightening and stressful situations have been worsened for spousal equivalents by the denial of a decision-making role. They have seen family members who have refused to allow one spousal equivalent visiting rights with another.

USA Today ran a story on July 2, 1990, which illustrates the worst case scenario for spousal equivalents. A lesbian couple, who were never advised to protect themselves with powers of attorney or wills, fought a five year battle for legal recognition of their relationship following a 1983 car accident which left one of them brain-damaged. The injured woman's father refused to let her spousal equivalent visit or have any say in medical treatment. The National Organization of Women presented the two women with their 1990 Women of Courage Award, and recognized their efforts to educate others to make the legal system work for them, not against them.

The medical power of attorney is a recent development in response to the needs of spousal equivalents, and should be seriously considered. An attorney can inform you of the requirements and your state's recognition of such a document.

Living Wills

In a July 1990 ruling, the Supreme Court indirectly supported the concept of a living will when the family of a comatose Missouri woman was denied the right to terminate treatment because the woman had not made her wishes known. The inference made by the court was that a person who had executed a living will would give her doctor or family the right to refuse treatment. (In a later ruling, the court heard evidence from a friend that the woman had expressed her desire to have treatment terminated if she should ever be in such a situation. Her family was finally given the right to take her off the machines which were keeping her alive.)

A living will gives a person the right to spell out how much medical care—if any—they want if they become critically or terminally ill and can no longer make their wishes known. Such a document must be unambiguous, and the determination by two physicians that the patient's condition is terminal is usually required. Forty-one states and the District of Columbia have specific statutes addressing this issue. Massachusetts, Michigan, New York, New Jersey, Ohio, Pennsylvania, Rhode Island and South Dakota do not have specific laws regarding living wills.

ADVICE FOR NON-DINKS*   12

DINKS: Acronym for couples who have "double income, no kids."

Statistically, the majority of couples who choose not to marry do not have children in the home. However, in this society of blended families, there are plenty of "yours, mine and ours" situations facing spousal equivalents. It is not uncommon for same sex couples to have offspring from prior opposite sex relationships. Children create their own special problems in a spousal equivalent relationship.

"Yours"

Typically, as in the case of William and Mary, the man's children live with their mother. This means that, although there is no child in the home on a full time basis, Mary must make compromises when William's son visits. Mary has no children of her own and has spent little time around children, but establishing a relationship with William also meant establishing a relationship with his son, Sam.

Luckily, Sam is a bright, attractive and well-behaved child. But that doesn't mean that Mary has not had her share of "you can't tell me what to do, you're not my mommy" situations during William's periods of visitation with Sam.

"Social parenting" is the term that has been created for the relationship spousal equivalents have with their partner's children. Though such relationships may suffer from the fact that the spousal equivalent has shaky status as an authority figure, these unwed "step-parents" often develop close and loving relationships with the children.

Even though there may be strong bonds, however, the spousal equivalent has no legal rights, obligations or privileges in a child's life upon separation or death of a partner. As Mary becomes more and more attached to Sam, she often remembers a friend who told her that the breakup with her boyfriend was not as bad as the fact that she was no longer able to continue her relationship with his children.

The issue of child-support may become clouded when a father lives with a woman outside wedlock. Some states have taken the position that, upon re-marriage, a new spouse's income can be factored into increases in child support for children from a previous marriage; some states have ruled that it cannot be considered. However, it is now possible that some states will look at the finances of a household where the couples are spousal equivalents, and use the second income as a factor in setting child support.

In some situations, couples do live together when one or the other has children in the home. Studies seem to indicate that children who live in a home with their parent's spousal equivalent have more adjustment problems than those whose parents remain single or remarry. "The best interest of the child" is the critical issue in the determination of custody in most states. It is not unusual for a father to bring a suit for custody of his children when the mother is living with someone.

Consenting adults should have the freedom to chose their marital status. But a parent with custody of children may be risking the privilege of retaining that custody. The impact on both the children and the spousal equivalent cannot be minimized. There are no simple social or legal answers to these problems.

"Mine"

Nick and Nora have also dealt with the issue of children in their relationship. Although Nick is fairly conservative, and was a little uncertain about just living with Nora, he did not want to take on the responsibility, financial or otherwise, of her three almost-grown children. He raised children of his own and didn't want to deal with those problems again.

Although he is supportive of Nora, and genuinely likes her children, he prefers to be a friend and not a quasi-parent to them. Nora, on the other hand, is well aware that she would face problems with financial aid at college if she added Nick's income to her own, as well losing her alimony upon remarriage. Their arrangement suits them both fine, and has not created problems for any of their children.

"Ours"

Under English common law, an illegitimate child had no legal rights. Such a child was a *filius nullius,* a child of no one, neither father nor mother. Today's legal trend is to attempt to place all children on an equal footing, even though social discrimination may still exist.

The Uniform Parentage Act was approved by the American Bar Association in 1974. The theory behind this act is full equality for children in their legal relationship with both parents, whatever their marital status. Many states have adopted these guidelines, and many more follow them.

If the parents of a child marry at any time, the child becomes legitimate, no matter how old he is. If marriage is not in the picture, it is a wise parent who will determine the law of their home state, and take the proper steps to protect both parent and child. Despite the liberal legal stance, two spousal equivalents who bring a child into the world should be aware of some of the possible legal ramifications.

Although at common law a child was not even legally the child of the mother, this is not true today. Most states recognize the legal relationship between a mother and a child born out of wedlock. The father and child relationship may not be so simple, though, as parentage can be more difficult to determine.

In some states, placing the father's name on the birth certificate may be sufficient to establish this legal relationship. However, federal guidelines may be more stringent. Obtaining benefits from a deceased father's estate may require actual residence with a child born out of wedlock, or proof that the father was the child's primary means of support. Inheriting from a parent who dies without a will is virtually impossible if paternity was not determined while the man was alive.

A natural father runs the risk of having a child placed for adoption and losing the right to obtain custody of a child if his rights are not protected. Some form of voluntary legitimation of the child through the court system, depending on the state, is a good idea for both parents and child.

Agree, for the law is costly.

William Camden

One of the most critical factors in preparing your own cohabitation agreement is the timing. Don't wait until you need one. Don't wait until there is a misunderstanding or potential problems in your relationship to discuss these troublesome practical matters. Remember, as the level of love decreases, the level of selfishness increases.

Unfortunately, procrastination is a peculiarly human trait. If nothing else, discuss such an agreement with your spousal equivalent in the abstract. If we decided to make an agreement, what would we put in it? Such a discussion is almost guaranteed to make you realize that there are areas that need further analysis and further negotiation.

The following checklist is a starting point. Once you decide to formalize a contract, photocopy it and take it to the attorney of your choice.

When couples marry, they are, figuratively, handed a contract by the state. Remember, you have a blank slate. Be creative, be generous, and be thorough.

COHABITATION AGREEMENT CHECKLIST

SPOUSAL EQUIVALENT #1

Full Name _____

Home Address _____

City, State, Zip_____

Telephone_____

Business Address_____

Telephone_____

Social Security Number_____

SPOUSAL EQUIVALENT #2

Full Name _____

Home Address _____

City, State, Zip_____

Telephone_____

Business Address_____

Telephone_____

Social Security Number_____

1. Is either party currently legally married to a third

    party?_____

2. Date of commencement of cohabitation:

    _____

    _____

    NOTES:_____

    _____

    _____

3. Location of cohabitation_____

    a. apartment

        ☐ #1 on lease;

        ☐ #2 on lease;

        ☐ both cohabitants on lease;

        ☐ other.

    b. home (condominium,townhomes,etc.)

        ☐ rented (check applicable lease
           information above);

        ☐ owned by #1;

☐ owned by #2:

☐ owned by both as

   ☐ tenants in common;
   ☐ joint tenants;
   ☐ don't know.

☐ other.

NOTES: _____

_____

_____

_____

4. Is either cohabitant a student?_____

_____

_____

5. Does either cohabitant own his own business?

_____

_____

NOTES:_____

_____

_____

6. Do you plan to

    ☐ pool your earnings;

    ☐ maintain separate accounts;

    ☐ maintain a joint account for household

    expenses?

7. Do you have an estimated division of basic

    monthly living expenses?

    _____

    _____

    _____

    _____

8. Do you intend to spell out household

    responsibilities?

    _____

    If so, how will they be divided?

    _____

    _____

9. Do you own any joint property at this time other than a residence?

_____

_____

_____

_____

_____

_____

10. Do you have any joint debts at this time other than a mortgage?

_____

_____

Spousal Equivalent #1

11. Do you have a last will and testament?_____

_____

_____

12. Do you have a current policy of life insurance?

_____

_____

_____

_____

NOTES: _____

_____

_____

_____

_____

Attach a current financial statement as Exhibit A to this checklist. Also, attach a current list of separate property assets and debts as Exhibit B.

Spousal Equivalent #2

13. Do you have a last will and testament?_____

_____

_____

_____

_____

14. Do you have a current policy of life insurance?

_____

_____

NOTES: _____

_____

_____

_____

Attach a current financial statement as Exhibit C to this checklist. Also, attach a current list of separate property assets and debts as Exhibit D.

15. Do either of you intend to make provisions for support after termination of the relationship?

_____

_____

NOTES: _____

_____

_____

_____

16. Do either of you have separate property which you intend to classify as joint property at this time?

_____

_____

_____

NOTES:_____

_____

17. Do either of you have minor children?_____

If yes,

   □ do the children live with you?;

   □ is there a need for support from one partner?;

   □ is there a possibility of adoption?;

   □ do the children own significant property in their own rights?

NOTES:

_____

_____

18. Do provisions need to be spelled out regarding birth control and addressing the issues of any potential children born to your relationship?

_____

_____

_____

NOTES:_____

_____

_____

_____

_____

_____

_____

After presenting this form to an attorney, discuss the laws on cohabitation in your state, i.e. criminal penalties and current view towards cohabitation agreements.

How to Find An Attorney

It is a fact of life that attorneys are expensive. But legal fees can be surprisingly reasonable for basic services such as preparation of a simple will or a deed to property.

Fees become exorbitant when matters are contested, and preventing such a situation is the reason to prepare a cohabitation agreement. If you follow the advice in this book, and know what you want and don't want before you even approach an attorney, the cost should be within any spousal equivalent's budget.

Our favorite story about legal fees comes from Richard Alderman, an attorney and professor of law at the University of Houston, as well as a television personality known as "The People's Lawyer" on the local NBC station. Richard called a variety of law firms for quotes on the cost of preparing a simple will for a single man who wanted to leave his estate to his parents. Richard was quoted prices ranging from $35.00 to $750.00. The moral of this story: comparison shopping will teach you more than you want to know about attorneys' fees.

The best way to find an attorney is through a referral from someone you know. Make sure, however, that these referrals have some expertise in the area about which you are calling. An attorney who handled an auto accident case for a friend may know nothing of family law. You are not looking merely for reputation, but for personal experience.

If you are unable to obtain a personal recommendation, there are a variety of other means to locate an attorney:

☞ Lawyer Referral Services of local and state bar associations;

☞ Martindale-Hubble Law Directory at your library, which lists education, affiliations, areas of expertise and biographical data of members of the bar throughout the U.S.;

☞ advertisements.

When dealing with a referral service, ask questions about qualifications required before a lawyer is listed as a family law practitioner. Referral services usually require that the attorney charge a minimal fee for consultations. Martindale-Hubble can give you basic information, but may not help in narrowing your selection.

Advertisements are riskier than the other two alternatives, but interviewing the lawyer about experience in the family law area and asking for references will protect you if you use this method.

Many states have procedures that an attorney may follow to become a specialist in a certain area of law. Legal specialization means that an attorney has met specific requirements and passed a written test through the State Bar Association. Attorneys who specialize have higher hourly rates, so this is not the only criteria you need to be aware when making a decision.

Small, medium or large?

A big firm is perfect for big clients with big problems that cover a variety of areas of law. Big firms usually work for business clients. The disadvantages of a big firm are high overhead costs and the very real possibility that you may pay the legal costs of a partner when a lawyer not long out of law school actually handles the work on your case.

A medium firm will cost less and often provide more personalized service. However, the small firm or sole practitioner is more likely to concentrate on individuals or small businesses than either the medium or large firm. Most lawyers who specialize in family law tend to be either sole practitioners or in small firms.

A sole practitioner can probably handle most of the basics of a spousal equivalent situation. Wills, powers of attorney, deeds and preparation of a cohabitation agreement are all well within the range of a sole practitioner who is familiar with family law. If not, a sole practitioner should be willing to refer you to an attorney with the necessary expertise, much as a family doctor would.

Remember, the attorney works for you. Once you have narrowed down your choices, call the office of each attorney and ask about the possibility of a brief, free consultation. If this is not available, make sure you are aware of the charge for the consultation before going in for an appointment. If you are being billed hourly for the consultation, be prepared to use this time wisely.

Now that you've found one...

You need a lawyer who will both listen to you and talk to you...in English, not legalese.   Rapport is important, and will be easier to establish if you are open and honest about your situation.   While the attorney is interviewing you, conduct your own interview.

Ask the lawyer the following questions and, if the answers are open and honest, you are on your way.

☞ What is your educational background?

☞ What is your main area of expertise?

☞ Will you personally handle my case, or will someone else be working on it with you?

☞ Do you employ paralegals, and if so, will their use reduce the amount of my bill?

☞ How much and on what basis do you charge, and can you give me an estimate of my final bill?

☞ Will there be a problem having my telephone calls returned?

☞ Why should I choose you over the other lawyers that have been recommended to me?

The biggest complaint about lawyers is that they don't return telephone calls. You want someone who understands that you want your calls to be returned promptly, but you should also be understanding about the realities of an attorney's day. You don't call your doctor and expect him to come to the telephone. An attorney is in court, interviewing clients, dictating and preparing documents, and sometimes it is impossible to handle every telephone call on the same day. When the staff tells you the attorney is in trial, be particularly patient.

Let the attorney know how important it is to you to have your calls returned promptly, and discuss the situation realistically in your initial interview. You want someone who isn't too busy to handle your needs, but you don't want someone who has too much time on their hands. Ask what you can expect, and if there is a particular staff member who can help if you cannot reach the attorney.

For preparation of the documents you need, the attorney should be able to quote a flat fee. Although it is possible the attorney may never have prepared a cohabitation agreement, you know from this book what you need. Knowledge of basic contract law principles and its applications to family law are the starting point. After that, don't expect the attorney to have all the answers immediately.

Let the attorney know that familiarity with the latest cases regarding cohabitants in your jurisdiction, as well as the trend of national cases, is one of your areas of concern. The attorney should be aware of the risk of self-incrimination resulting from signing an agreement which says you live with someone in states where there are still laws against such behavior.

To accomplish these ends, the attorney will likely need to do some research. Ask if this work can also be billed as a flat fee. When an attorney is learning a new area of expertise which can be used in the future, a compromise on the cost is not unreasonable.

The only aspect of creating a cohabitation agreement which is an exception to a flat fee arrangement is the fact that another attorney must be involved in reviewing the document for your spousal equivalent. Two lawyers have the potential of creating an adversarial situation.

Assure your attorney this is not going to happen, but that you will be responsible for any additional fees involved if unexpected problems arise. Then do everything possible to prevent this.

In drawing up your cohabitation agreement, both attorneys should be merely formalizing the deal the spousal equivalents have reached together. Neither lawyer should be involved in actually doing the deal. All you are asking is that all the bases are covered in making your agreement legally valid.

Neither spousal equivalent wants this situation to create antagonism. There are areas in your agreement which will rely on trust, goodwill and common sense. You and your spousal equivalent are preparing this agreement with the knowledge that you both have a little class. Show sophistication in asking the pertinent questions, and let your attorneys know that you don't want any more lawyering than in necessary.

Don't allow either lawyer to gum up the works. Both spousal equivalents should look on the positive side, let the lawyers look on the negative side, and settle for a compromise between the two.

And without a cohabitation agreement?

It is possible to take two opposing views of our laws. They are for the protection of society and its members, but they are often frequently viewed as a means of oppression. The fact that laws remain on the books today making it a criminal offense for consenting adults to cohabit is an example. The existence of laws prohibiting certain sexual acts between consenting adults remains a reality for same sex couples in a number of states.

Lawsuits and the court system are expensive, time consuming, and often inscrutable to the average person. It is important to understand what your rights are under the current laws, and to apply this knowledge to protect yourself. This knowledge will allow you to approach your situation with common sense, and the goal of avoiding conflicts and, ultimately, the courthouse. We want to help you beat the high cost of falling in and out of love.

The time, money and emotional agony of litigation are often fruitless investments. We want you to avoid these problems—no one wins in litigated family cases except the lawyers. The pain and anger take their toll and can be even more significant than the financial loss. A spousal equivalent bent on revenge is only hurting himself.

If you find yourself in a contested situation with your spousal equivalent, a court battle is a roll of the dice. Rarely is it possible for a judge or jury, in a matter of hours, to dispense justice in a situation which may have taken years to develop. Individuals lose their identities in a courtroom, and outcomes are notoriously hard to predict.

There is less financial stress and emotional pain in a negotiated settlement. Anger and guilt either one are bad for your bank account. Both are overreactions to an emotional situation. In a negotiated settlement, you can both win. Taking a case to court, you both lose.

THE LAST CHAPTER 14

"He who hesitates is not only lost, but miles from the next exit."

Unknown

The first challenge for any couple, married or single, is finding a way to live happily together. The everyday trial and error, success and failure, of a relationship is equally difficult no matter what your marital status.

In closing, we want to re-emphasize the importance of diminishing the hurdles which face spousal equivalents in particular. The majority of the problems addressed in previous chapters have dealt with one of the two biggest problems in any relationship, the f-word: finances. We will leave advice on the sexual issues to specialists in that area.

Following is our re-cap of advice to each of the four couples introduced as examples. Hopefully, every spousal equivalent can see parallels to their own situation in these scenarios, and shape this advice to their own needs.

William and Mary

William and Mary are the only couple out of the four who have actually executed a cohabitation agreement. As successful business people, they understand the necessity of reducing understandings to writing. They feel that their relationship has been made stronger by the discussion and negotiation required to complete their agreement. Both have a realistic picture of their relationship, and do not feel that this has spoiled the romance.

This couple has also arranged life insurance policies which will protect the other in the event of a death of either partner. However, William's previous will was executed prior to the birth of his son. It made provisions for his estate to go to his ex-wife, provisions which are now void because of the divorce. He never executed another because of the adjustment necessary in the family when Sam was born, and then because of the marital problems which led to his divorce. He knows that he needs to prepare a new will, but has not taken care of the matter.

Mary has never executed a will and also realizes that this is something important she needs to do. Also, it would be a good idea if durable and medical powers of attorney were executed at the same time as their wills.

William and Mary both have accountants and have consulted a financial planner and are sophisticated enough in these matters that any further advice is redundant.

Nick and Nora

Nick and Nora each have a current will. Nick made provisions in his will for Nora to have a "life estate" in his home. This will allow her to live in the house until her death, but gives her no financial interest in the property to the detriment of his children.

They have also signed durable and medical powers of attorney. Nick made his daughter Mary his attorney-in-fact for financial matters, as he felt his children would object if he allowed Nora to handle his personal affairs in the event of his disability. Nora, however, does not feel her children are sufficiently mature to take on this obligation for her, so she asked Nick to serve in this capacity.

However, in reference to medical powers of attorney, they have put this responsibility on each other. Their children are sufficiently busy with their own lives, and Nick and Nora feel that part of their commitment to each other is to care for the other in the event of illness. This is something they have discussed in depth, and both feel that the other knows their wishes in these matters. Their children would be uncomfortable dealing with these issues, but Nick and Nora are realistic enough to know that illness and death are inevitable and they want nothing left to chance.

Pat and Mike

Looking at Pat and Mike's situation from one standpoint, they have the least potential for legal and financial problems of all of these couples. They have few assets and little earning power. Their energies are focused primarily on finishing their educations and then getting married.

But there are problems facing them when the status of one or the other changes. They are living in the state that handed down the *Hewitt* decision. At this time, they are not sure who will enter the work force first and who will continue an education. It is not likely that they will enter the business world and leave academia behind at the same time. If they do marry, they are not sure exactly when this event will take place.

If Pat and Mike continue their cohabitation past their college years, the risks become greater. Obviously, neither wants to spend their limited funds on an attorney or financial planner at this point. If nothing else, executing a cohabitation agreement when one enters the work force would be wise, particularly if the actual wedding date is still uncertain at that time.

Wills would be beneficial for this couple as well. It is never too early to execute a will. It is imperative to do so after the birth of a child. In the event of the death of parents, a will names a trustee to handle financial affairs for a child and a guardian to actually care for the child. It also establishes guidelines for these parties in overseeing both the person and the estate of the child.

The statistical probabilities of death or disability to this young couple are obviously smaller than to the other couples, but tragedy can strike at any age. Total protection could be achieved for Pat and Mike if they execute a cohabitation agreement, wills, and durable and medical powers of attorney. Also, life insurance premiums are based on the age of the insured, and lower rates would be available to them at this time.

As far as financial planning advice, a basic plan of opening two IRA's as soon as possible would make this couple financially secure at age 65. As is the case with most young couples, finding money for savings will be difficult and not high on their list of priorities in the first few years out of school. But as practical, basic advice, they should consider finding a way to accomplish this goal.

Bob and Ted

Bob and Ted have more resources than any of our other couples. They do not have a cohabitation agreement, but they do have durable and medical powers of attorney. Bob has executed a will. Ted does not think he needs one.

As we covered in the chapter on planning for death and disability, the size of your estate is not the issue in determining your need for a will. Even if all you own is a used car, the issue of how to transfer its title could cost as much as the car is worth. Ted needs to execute a will.

A cohabitation agreement is recommended in this relationship. Bob has enough resources to make him a target, particularly in California, for a "palimony" suit if he left Ted. Ted, if he left Bob, would be abandoning a very comfortable lifestyle and potentially losing compensation for his efforts in renovating and maintaining Bob's properties. They both stand to lose.

Because they live in a progressive state, a claim by either of these men would most likely be upheld in court. Many states, however, are not as sympathetic to lesbian and gay issues as California. Depending on the state of residence, same sex couples who are involved in business ventures together might consider forming a business partnership as well as protecting themselves with a cohabitation agreement. Courts can uphold business contracts without moral issues becoming involved.

The Last Word

As pointed out in our introduction, our goal has been to show you how to protect yourself and your partner from the real world realities that can interfere with your romance. Our couples were created with the hope that any spousal equivalent reading this book could relate to these fictional situations in their own life.

This guide is only a starting point, however, and it is a work in progress. As the laws change, and as we hear from more and more spousal equivalents with their questions and ideas, we'll get back to you with more information.

In the meantime, please remember that this book is general in nature. As we have stated throughout these chapters, every state is different. Please consult an attorney, accountant or financial planner in your area to apply this information to the practical issues in your own relationship.

Appendix A

The following is an overview of the law as of 1990 in each of the following states. **Do not** *depend on the information in this appendix without consulting an attorney in your home state. Liberal vs. conservative and urban vs. rural jurisdictions differ within each state, and may have an impact on the outcome of a particular fact situation. The effect of cohabitation on alimony is only addressed if there is an appropriate law or case on that subject in the state.*

ALABAMA

Can residents enter into an informal marriage?   Yes

Is it a crime to live together?   No

Theory of marital property: Separate

Effect of cohabitation on alimony:

Statute provides alimony terminable upon proof that recipient is living openly with a member of the opposite sex.

Most significant case for spousal equivalents:

In *Albae vs. Harmon,* 30 So.2d 459 (Ala.1947), the court affirmed a resulting trust of two parcels of land for a woman who cohabitated with a man. The court felt that the woman was entitled to equity when it was shown that, although the title was taken in the man's name alone, she had paid the entire purchase price of the property with her own money.

ALASKA

Can residents enter into an informal marriage?   No

Is it a crime to live together?   No

Theory of marital property: Separate

Most significant case for spousal equivalents:

Levar vs. Elkins, 604 P.2d 602 (Alaska 1980), was a suit by a woman who had lived with a man for twenty years in a nonmarital union. Her award of $15,000 based on a contract theory of recovery was upheld.

ARIZONA

Can residents enter into an informal marriage?   No

Is it a crime to live together?   Yes

Theory of marital property: Community

Effect of cohabitation on alimony:

Case law indicates that alimony will not be terminated because of cohabitation.

Most significant case for spousal equivalents:

Cook vs. Cook, 691 P.2d 664 (Ariz. 1984), and *Carroll vs. Lee,* 712 P.2d 923 (Ariz. 1986) are the two leading cases. Cook established that Arizona would uphold an implied partnership agreement between cohabitants. Carroll extended this position by upholding an implied contract.

ARKANSAS

Can residents enter into an informal marriage?   No

Is it a crime to live together?   No

Theory of marital property: Separate

Most significant case for spousal equivalents:

Mitchell vs. Fish, 134 S.W. 940 (Ark.1911), was an early forerunner of *Marvin.* The court held that, in an action by a woman who had left her husband and gone with defendant and lived with him as his wife, she was entitled to a division of property. The fact that her actions were tainted with immorality did not make such a division illegal. The court felt that this was not a question of public policy, but whether one partner, having received profits of partnership property, was liable to another for an agreed division.

CALIFORNIA

Can residents enter into an informal marriage?   **No**

Is it a crime to live together?   **No**

Theory of marital property: Community

Effect of cohabitation on alimony:

Statute provides for a presumption of decreased need upon proof of cohabitation with member of opposite sex.

Most significant case for spousal equivalents:

The *Marvin* case, 557 P. 2d 106 (Cal. 1976), is discussed at length in the text. As a footnote to that case, Marvin Mitchelson was sanctioned by the California Court of Appeals and fined $15,000 for what the court considered a frivolous appeal in a palimony suit.

In a leading same sex case, *Conley vs. Richardson*, a lesbian couple ended their relationship and one partner was ordered to pay the other temporary support. The couple had a written agreement in addition to an implied oral agreement under the principles of *Marvin.* As usual, the state of California leads the way in rights for spousal equivalents.

COLORADO

Can residents enter into an informal marriage?   Yes

Is it a crime to live together   No

Theory of marital property: Separate

Effect of cohabitation on alimony:

Case law requires a "holding-out" as husband and wife before cohabitation will be grounds to terminate alimony.

Most significant case for spousal equivalents:

As Colorado recognizes common-law marriage, there appears to be no relevant case on property division based on cohabitation alone. However, *In re Marriage of Blietz,* 538 P. 2d 114 (Colo. 1975), a property division was upheld after the annulment of a marriage. The court awarded all property acquired with the woman's funds to the woman, despite the fact that title was actually in both parties as joint tenants. Early case law suggests that a contract based only on sexual services, however, would be void.

CONNECTICUT

Can residents enter into an informal marriage?   No

(It is possible that an informal marriage contracted outside the state would not be upheld in Connecticut.)

Is it a crime to live together?   No

Theory of marital property: Separate

Effect of cohabitation on alimony:

Alimony may be modified if the recipient's living arrangements cause such a change of circumstances as to alter the financial needs of the party.

Most significant case for spousal equivalents:

Boland vs. Catalano, 521 A.2d 142 (Conn. 1987), held that rights and obligations of a valid marriage do not arise from cohabitation, but that ordinary contract principles are not suspended for unmarried persons living together, whether or not they engage in sexual activity.

DELAWARE

Can residents enter into an informal marriage?   No

Is it a crime to live together?   No

Theory of marital property: Separate

Effect of cohabitation on alimony:

Case law indicates that alimony may be terminated for cohabitation.

Most significant case for spousal equivalents:

Siple vs. Corbett, 447 A.2d 1184 (Del. 1962), held that a contract founded upon consideration for romantic involvements including sexual favors was void as against public policy and unenforceable by the courts. Decided before the *Marvin* decision, it is not clear whether equitable principles or a written cohabitation agreement would prevail in Delaware.

DISTRICT OF COLUMBIA

Can residents enter into an informal marriage?   Yes

Is it a crime to live together?   No

Theory of marital property: Separate

Most significant case for spousal equivalents:

Coleman vs. Jackson, 286 F.2d 98 (App. D. C., 1977), held that parties in an illicit relationship could hold property jointly and give or bequeath property to each other without limitations imposed because of their relationship.

FLORIDA

Can residents enter into an informal marriage?   No

Is it a crime to live together?   Yes

Theory of marital property: Separate

Effect of cohabitation on alimony:

Florida courts have held that cohabitation is not grounds for terminating alimony.

Most significant case for spousal equivalents:

Poe vs. Levy, 411 So.2d 253 (Fla. Dist. Ct. App. 1982), held that a cause of action based on an express contract or for construction of a trust is enforceable regardless of the fact that the parties were cohabitants as long as there was valid, lawful consideration separate and apart from an agreement regarding sexual services. *Evans v. Wall*, 15 F.L.R. 1374 (Fla. Dist. Ct. App. 1989) ordered a monetary award under a constructive trust or equitable lien theory in favor of an unmarried cohabitant who had contributed funds and services to the other cohabitant's residential and commercial property during a five year period.

GEORGIA

Can residents enter into an informal marriage?   Yes

Is it a crime to live together?   No

Theory of marital property?   Separate

Effect of cohabitation on alimony:

Statute provides that alimony may be modified if recipient spouse is living with a member of the opposite sex in a meretricious relationship.

Most significant case for spousal equivalents:

In *Rehak vs. Mathis,* 238 S.E. 2d 81 (Georgia, 1977), the Georgia Supreme Court refused to allow a woman who had cohabited with a man for 18 years to recover a share of jointly acquired property. The court held that it could not uphold a contract founded on illegal or immoral consideration.

HAWAII

Can residents enter into an informal marriage?   No

Is it a crime to live together?   No

Theory of marital property: Separate

Most significant case for spousal equivalents:

In *Artiss vs. Artiss,* 8 FLR 2313 (Hawaii, 1982), the court found "a sufficient familial relationship" to allow a division of property acquired by an unmarried couple who had lived together 24 years. The court cited *Marvin* in the decision.

IDAHO

Can residents enter into an informal marriage?   Yes

Is it a crime to live together?   Yes

Theory of marital property: Community

Most significant case for spousal equivalents:

In *Curtis vs. Curtis*, 15 FLR 1023 (Idaho 1988), Sandra Curtis filed suit against Carl Curtis and the court found that he had expressly or impliedly agreed to "take care of" her. The order of the court was that Carl pay Sandra's school expenses, attorney's fees, and dental expenses, as well as six months of support (unless she got married.)

ILLINOIS

Can residents enter into an informal marriage?   No

Is it a crime to live together?   Yes

Theory of marital property: Separate

Effect of cohabitation on alimony:

By statute, alimony may be terminated for cohabitation on a "continuing, conjugal basis."

Most significant case for spousal equivalents:

Hewitt vs. Hewitt, 394 N.E. 2d 1204 (Ill. 1979) is discussed at length in the text has not been overturned in Illinois. However, in *Staff vs. Estate of Nottolini,* 13 FLR 1333, (Ill. 1987), a recovery by a woman who had served as nurse for her cohabitant was upheld against his estate. The court's rationale was the lack of sexual services involved in the relationship, due to the man's ill health. The court used the theories of implied or express agreement and quantum meruit.

INDIANA

Can residents enter into an informal marriage?   No
Is it a crime to live together?   No

Theory of marital property: Separate

Most significant case for spousal equivalents:

In *Glasgo vs. Glasgo,* 410 N.E. 2d 1325, (Ind. App., 1980), an ex-husband appealed a judgment giving his ex-wife a share of property acquired during their cohabitation prior to marriage. The court felt that the a claim was not against public policy and held that the property acquired prior to marriage should be shared. The court also upheld a division of property acquired before marriage in a divorce case in *Chestnut vs. Chestnut*, 13 FLR 1077, (Ind. App., 1986).

IOWA

Can residents enter into an informal marriage?   Yes

Is it a crime to live together?   No

Theory of marital property: Separate

Most significant case for spousal equivalents:

In *Shold vs. Goro*, 16 FLR 1104, (Iowa Sup. Ct., 1989), the court upheld a repayment of loans from one spousal equivalent to another. The unjust enrichment theory was applied. In another decision, *In re Freel*, 16 FLR 1070, the court overruled the right of visitation granted to a woman with her former spousal equivalent's son.

KANSAS

Can residents enter into an informal marriage?   Yes

Is it a crime to live together?   No

Theory of marital property: Separate

Most significant case for spousal equivalents:

In *Eaton vs. Johnson*, 681 P. 2d 606 (Kan. 1984), the court found that it was authorized to make an equitable division of property accumulated during cohabitation once cohabitation ended.

KENTUCKY

Can residents enter into an informal marriage?   No

Is it a crime to live together?   No

Theory of marital property: Separate

Effect of cohabitation on alimony:

Case law permits reduction of alimony because of cohabitation under certain circumstances.

Most significant case for spousal equivalents:

As early as 1851, a Kentucky court in *McDonald vs. Fleming*, 51 Ky. 285 (Ky. 1851), held that money lent by a mistress to her lover to acquire title to land in his name alone could be recovered using an equitable lien on the property. In *Cougler vs. Fackler*, 510 S.W. 2d 1974 (Ky. App. 1974), the existence of a meretricious relationship did not bar a man from recovering from a woman when she broke an oral promise to deed land to him in exchange for money.

LOUISIANA

Can residents enter into an informal marriage?   **No**

Is it a crime to live together?   **No**

Theory of marital property: Community

Effect of cohabitation on alimony:

Alimony terminates if the recipient enters into "open concubinage."

Most significant case for spousal equivalents:

Louisiana law strongly urges the drafting of business partnerships instead of cohabitation agreements. Cases such as *Foshee vs. Simkin*, 174 So. 2d 915 (La. 1965), *Schwegman vs. Schwegman*, 441 So. 2d 316, (La. App. 1980), and *Jenkins vs. Provost*, 140 So. 2d 238, (La. App. 1962), follow the theory that parties who cohabit cannot assert a claim based on their illicit relationship, but may assert a claim arising out of a business relationship, where there is strict and conclusive proof that such a relationship existed. Also, there are restrictions on the amount and type of property which can be willed to a spousal equivalent.

MAINE

Can residents enter into an informal marriage?   No

Is it a crime to live together?   No

Theory of marital property: Separate

Most significant case for spousal equivalents:

In *Libby vs. Lorrain,* 430 A.2d 37 (Maine 1981), the court awarded a partition of real property owned by two cohabitants without addressing the meretricious nature of their relationship.

MARYLAND

Can residents enter into an informal marriage?   No

Is it a crime to live together?   No

Theory of marital property: Separate

Most significant case for spousal equivalents:

In *Donovan vs. Scuderi,* 443 A. 2d 121 (Md. 1982), the court held that a spousal equivalent situation, even if proven adulterous, did not disable the parties from making an enforceable contract with each other as long as the contract did not stand or fall upon their sexual relationship.

MASSACHUSETTS

Can residents enter into an informal marriage?   **No**

Is it a crime to live together?   **No**

Theory of marital property: Separate

Most significant case for spousal equivalents:

Sullivan v. Rooney, 15 FLR 1266 (Mass. 1989), found that a woman, who had lived with a man for several years outside marriage, was entitled to a one-half interest in a home that was titled in his name alone. The parties had considered the house a joint purchase, but placed title in the man's name because of financing. The man paid the mortgage, taxes, utilities, and insurance on the house; the woman put all her earnings and savings into the home, paying for food and household supplies and much of the furniture. The court found that the woman had remained with the man based on his promise to convey joint title to the property and that he had induced her to contribute her earnings and savings to her detriment. The court imposed a constructive trust in her favor for one-half the property.

MICHIGAN

Can residents enter into an informal marriage?   **No**

Is it a crime to live together?   **Yes**

Theory of marital property: Separate

Effect of cohabitation on alimony:

Cohabitation is not sufficient to terminate alimony absent a showing of changed circumstances.

Most significant case for spousal equivalents:

Carnes vs. Sheldon, 311 N. W. 2d 747 (Mich. App. 1981) cited previously in the text, took a firm position that the legislature should determine the rights of cohabitating couples, and in this particular case, allowed no property division based on the facts presented. However, it did state that cohabitation did not render all agreements between parties illegal. Also, in *Tyranski vs. Piggins,* 205 N. W. 2d 595 (Mich., 1973), an oral promise to convey property to a cohabitant was upheld in a suit against the estate of the other cohabitant.

MINNESOTA

Can residents enter into an informal marriage?   No

Is it a crime to live together?   No

Theory of marital property: Separate

Most significant case for spousal equivalents:

The case of *Carlson vs. Olsen,* 256 N. W. 2d 249 (Minn. 1977), upheld the division of property acquired during a 21-year period of cohabitation when the evidence showed the parties had intended their accumulated property be divided equally. The court used the unusual theory that their contributions were gifts to each other that were irrevocable. Subsequently, the Minnesota legislature enacted a law in 1984 which requires cohabitation agreements (specifically, between a man and a woman) to be in writing.

MISSISSIPPI

Can residents enter into an informal marriage?   No

Is it a crime to live together?   Yes

Theory of marital property: Separate

Most significant case for spousal equivalents:

Contrary to the negative finding in the *Alexander* case, 445 So. 2d 836 (Miss. 1984), discussed in the text, the *Pickens vs. Pickens* decision, at 490 So. 2d 872 (Miss. 1986), upheld a division of property after a twenty year period of cohabitation. Holding that the relationship "must be acknowledged to be a partnership," the court said an "equitable division of such property will be ordered upon the permanent breakup and separation."

MISSOURI

Can residents enter into an informal marriage?   No

Is it a crime to live together?   No

Theory of marital property: Separate

Most significant case for spousal equivalents:

Hudson vs. Delonjay, 732 S.W. 2d 922 (Mo. App. 1987), upheld a division of property between two cohabitants, finding that public policy did not preclude the finding of an implied contract.

MONTANA

Can residents enter into an informal marriage?   Yes

Is it a crime to live together?   No

Theory of marital property: Separate

Most significant case for spousal equivalents:

No relevant case.

NEBRASKA

Can residents enter into an informal marriage?   No

Is it a crime to live together?   No

Theory of marital property: Separate

Effect of cohabitation on alimony:

Cohabitation alone is not enough to terminate alimony absent a showing of changed circumstances.

Most significant case for spousal equivalents:

In *Kinkenon v. Hue*, 301 N.W. 2d 77 (Nebraska, 1981), the court held that, upon a showing that sexual services were not the basis for an agreement, that a division of property between two cohabitants was not a violation of public policy.

NEVADA

Can residents enter into an informal marriage?   No

Is it a crime to live together?   No

Theory of marital property: Community

Most significant case for spousal equivalents:

Unmarried couples who are living together have the same rights to lawfully contract with each other regarding their property as do other unmarried people, according to the court's findings in *Hay vs. Hay*, 678 P. 2d 672 (Nev. 1984). The court also held that contracts could be either express or implied.

NEW HAMPSHIRE

Can residents enter into an informal marriage? Yes

Is it a crime to live together? No

Theory of marital property: Separate

Most significant case for spousal equivalents:

In the case of *Joan S. vs. John S.*, 498 A. 2d 498 (N.H.,1981), the court denied a finding of marriage between two cohabitating parties who sought a divorce, but implied that they would uphold a division of property and would follow Marvin if the facts supported such a finding.

NEW JERSEY

Can residents enter into an informal marriage? No

Is it a crime to live together? No

Theory of marital property: Separate

Most significant case for spousal equivalents:

Kozlowski v. Kozlowski, 403 A. 2d 902 (New Jersey, 1979) said that New Jersey public policy does not condemn cohabitation between a man and woman who are unmarried as meretricious. The court also stated that the decision to cohabit without marriage represents a person's voluntary choice and this is a choice with which the state should not interfere.

NEW MEXICO

Can residents enter into an informal marriage?   No

Is it a crime to live together?   No

Theory of marital property: Community

Most significant case for spousal equivalents:

Dominguez vs. Cruz, 7 FLR 2025 (N. M. Ct. App., 1980), the court upheld an oral agreement between two cohabitants to pool their acquired property. Citing *Marvin,* the court said that "if an agreement such as an oral contract can exist between two business associates, one can exist between two adults who are not married."

NEW YORK

Can residents enter into an informal marriage?   No

Is it a crime to live together?   No

Theory of marital property: Separate

Effect of cohabitation on alimony:

Alimony may be modified upon proof that wife is living with another man and holding herself out as his wife.

Most significant case for spousal equivalents:

New York recognizes express agreements, either written or oral, between two unmarried cohabitants as long as illicit sexual relations are not part of the agreement, *Morone vs. Morone,* 50 N.Y.S. 2d 481 (1980). The court rejected the *Marvin* concept of upholding an implied contract.

NORTH CAROLINA

Can residents enter into an informal marriage?   No

Is it a crime to live together?   Yes

Theory of marital property: Separate

Most significant case for spousal equivalents:

In *Collins vs. Davis,* 315 SE 2d 759 (N. C. App., 1984), it was held that the division of property between two cohabitants could be allowed, despite the fact that the man was legally married to someone else. The court held that, absent evidence that the man acted dishonestly or fraudulently, his "immoral" acts did not close the doors of law and equity to him.

NORTH DAKOTA

Can residents enter into an informal marriage?   No

Is it a crime to live together?   Yes

Theory of marital property: Separate

Most significant case for spousal equivalents:

No relevant case.

OHIO

Can residents enter into an informal marriage?   Yes

Is it a crime to live together?   No

Theory of marital property: Separate

Most significant case for spousal equivalents:

An Ohio court, in *Lauper vs. Harold*, 492 NE 2d 472 (Ohio App., 1985), stated that it was reluctant to create a precedent for allowing a division of property based on "mere" cohabitation, but could not allow unjust enrichment of one party at the expense of another. A division of property was granted to a female cohabitant against a male cohabitant.

OKLAHOMA

Can residents enter into an informal marriage?   Yes

Is it a crime to live together?   No

Theory of marital property: Separate

Effect of cohabitation on alimony:

Alimony may be modified if recipient cohabits with a member of the opposite sex.

Most significant case for spousal equivalents:

There is early authority on meretricious cohabitation which indicates that a contract may be upheld if not founded on the illicit nature of the relationship, *Emmerson vs. Botkin*, 26 Okla. 218 (Okla., 1910.) In *M. J. P. vs. J. G. P.*, 8 FLR 2217 (Okla., 1982), a mother's cohabitation with a female lover was sufficient evidence to award custody of children to father.

OREGON

Can residents enter into an informal marriage?   No

Is it a crime to live together?   No

Theory of marital property: Separate

Most significant case for spousal equivalents:

In a case of one woman suing her same sex cohabitant, *Ireland vs. Flanagan*, 627 P. 2d 496 (Oregon App., 1981), the court granted a division of property. The women bought a house together, titled in Flanagan's name. Because they had an agreement to pool their resources, the court found the women were tenants in common and awarded a split, proportionate with their contributions to the price of the house.

PENNSYLVANIA

Can residents enter into an informal marriage?   Yes

Is it a crime to live together?   No

Theory of marital property: Separate

Effect of cohabitation on alimony:

Alimony may be denied upon proof of cohabitation with member of the opposite sex who is not related.

Most significant case for spousal equivalents:

In *Knauer vs. Knauer*, 470 A. 2d 553 (Pennsylvania, 1983), the Superior Court found that a contract between cohabitating parties was valid, as long as it was not founded solely on the procurement of sexual services.

RHODE ISLAND

Can residents enter into an informal marriage?   Yes

Is it a crime to live together?   No

Theory of marital property: Separate

Effect of cohabitation on alimony:

Cohabitation not sufficient to terminate alimony without showing of changed economic circumstances.

Most significant case for spousal equivalents:

Although it appears that no case has upheld the property division of cohabitants in this state, it seems to be the fact situations which have failed to meet the criteria. The decisions seems to indicate that, with the proper facts, an agreement which was not based solely on sexual services would be upheld.

SOUTH CAROLINA

Can residents enter into an informal marriage?   Yes

Is it a crime to live together?   No

Theory of marital property: Separate

Most significant case for spousal equivalents:

In *Grant vs. Butt*, 17 S.E. 2d 689 (S. C., 1941), the court held that consideration of past cohabitation would be sufficient to sustain a contract, although a contract for future cohabitation, or a combination of past and future, was invalid.

SOUTH DAKOTA

Can residents enter into an informal marriage?   **No**

However, a South Dakota court did uphold a common-law marriage of a couple who were married, divorced, and then resumed living together without a formal ceremony.   Beuck v. Howe, 23 N.W. 2d 744 (S.D. 1946).

Is it a crime to live together?   **No**

Theory of marital property: **Separate**

Most significant case for spousal equivalents:

In the 1940's, in a very early forerunner of *Marvin*, *Beuck vs. Howe*, 23 N.W. 2d 744 (South Dakota 1946), the court held that the illicit relations of a man and woman who live together do not give rise to property rights, but property acquired through their joint efforts should be proportionately divided according to their contributions.

TENNESSEE

Can residents enter into an informal marriage?   No

Is it a crime to live together?   No

Theory of marital property: Separate

Most significant case for spousal equivalents:

Contracts for immoral purposes are not enforceable in Tennessee. In *Roach vs. Buttons*, 6 FLR 2355 (Tenn., 1980), a Tennessee court, stating that a couple's live-in relationship was "not sanctioned by Natural or Divine Law," refused to award equity relief to a woman seeking a claim after 15 months of cohabitation. However, the court used the theory of "compassion" to award her $3,000 to purchase a car because she had traded hers in to help purchase a car titled in her boyfriend's name alone. An early case in the state, however, indicates that a business relationship would be upheld despite illicit relations (*Johnson vs. Graves*, 15 Tenn. App. 466 (Tenn. 1932).

TEXAS

Can residents enter into an informal marriage?   Yes

Is it a crime to live together?   No

Theory of marital property: Community

Most significant case for spousal equivalents:

Sec. 26.01(a) of the Business & Commerce Code was enacted by the legislature in 1987 to restrict the abusive filing of palimony suits. It provides that a promise or agreement, including one made in consideration of nonmarital conjugal cohabitation, is not enforceable unless the promise or agreement, or a memorandum of it, is in writing and signed by the person to be charged with the promise or agreement. The effect of this legislation is to make recovery on oral agreements difficult.

Prior to this legislation, Texas had upheld claims in spousal equivalent situations on various theories of recovery, including the leading same sex case, *Small vs. Harper*, 638 S.W. 2d 24 (Tex. App. 1982), when a property division in an alleged lesbian relationship was upheld on theories of oral partnership, joint venture, and resulting and constructive trust theories. However, a written cohabitation agreement complying with the requirements of the legislation is to be urged.

UTAH

Can residents enter into an informal marriage?   Yes

Is it a crime to live together?   No

Theory of marital property: Separate

Effect of cohabitation on alimony:

Alimony terminates upon proof that recipient is residing with a member of the opposite sex, unless the relationship does not involve sexual contact.

Most significant case for spousal equivalents:

Edgar vs. Wagner, 572 P. 2d 405 (Utah, 1977), the court allowed a woman who had married a man, knowing he was already married, to recover a portion of the value of a house they shared, as well as a monetary award for the value of the service she had performed in helping the man run his business.

VERMONT

Can residents enter into an informal marriage?   **No**

Is it a crime to live together?   **No**

Theory of marital property: **Separate**

Most significant case for spousal equivalents:

In a very early recognition of the rights of spousal equivalents, Vermont decided in *Stewart vs. Waterman*, 123 A. 524 (Vt. 1924), that the mere existence of a meretricious relationship did not prohibit the parties from forming a contract.

VIRGINIA

Can residents enter into an informal marriage?   **No**

Is it a crime to live together?   Yes

This state statute has been declared unconstitutional, *Doe vs. Duling*, 603 F. Supp. 960 (E.D. Va. 1985), by a federal court, although it is still on the books.

Theory of marital property: Separate

Effect of cohabitation on alimony:

Case law does not support modification of alimony on proof of cohabitation.

Most significant case for spousal equivalents:

Although it does not deal with the division of property, the case of *Cord vs. Gibb*, 254 S. E. 2d 71 (Va. 1979), involved an applicant for the State Bar of Virginia who was originally denied the right to take the Virginia Bar examination due to her cohabitation with a member of the opposite sex. She won the right on appeal. There appears to be no relevant case on the issue of property division, probably due to the history of criminal penalties against cohabitation. However, now that the statute has been declared unconstitutional, the state is in a position to determine its stand on spousal equivalents.

WASHINGTON

Can residents enter into an informal marriage?   No

Is it a crime to live together?   No

Theory of marital property: Community

Effect of cohabitation on alimony:

A provision in a divorce decree which provided that alimony would terminate on cohabitation was improper, *In re Tower*, 15 FLR 1620 (Wash. 1989).

Most significant case for spousal equivalents:

The cases of *Antoine vs. Thornton*, 499 P. 2d 864 (Wash. 1972) and *Omer vs. Omer*, 523 P. 2d 957 (Wash. 1974) employed theories of implied partnership and constructive trusts to permit a division of property in long-term, stable nonmarital relationships.

WEST VIRGINIA

Can residents enter into an informal marriage?   No

Is it a crime to live together?   Yes

Theory of marital property: Separate

Most significant case for spousal equivalents:

No relevant case.

WISCONSIN

Can residents enter into an informal marriage?   No

Is it a crime to live together?   No

Theory of marital property: Community

Most significant case for spousal equivalents:

In *Watts vs. Watts*, 405 N.W. 2d 303 (Wis. 1987), the court held that nonmarital cohabitation did not render every agreement between cohabiting parties illegal and did not automatically preclude one party from seeking relief under contract law or equitable principles.

WYOMING

Can residents enter into an informal marriage?   No

Is it a crime to live together?   No

Theory of marital property: Separate

Most significant case for spousal equivalents:

Kinnison vs. Kinnison, 627 P. 2d 594 (Wyo. 1981), found that only when it is shown that an agreement between a man and woman living together has meretricious sexual services as its consideration will the court deny enforcement of agreement as being against public policy.

Appendix B

I. *Certified Financial Planner*

The designation "Certified Financial Planner" or "C.F.P." is reserved for those individuals who have completed a prescribed course of study. This course of study was originally administered and the designation awarded by the College for Financial Planning in Denver. Since 1985, the designation has been awarded by an independent governing board which also recognizes other approved financial planning programs. Candidates must demonstrate their proficiency by passing a series of written exams on such subjects as risk management, investments, taxation, retirement planning and estate planning.

In addition, a candidate must satisfy certain other criteria including actual work experience. Once awarded, in order to maintain the designation, the C.F.P. must also meet annual education requirements.

Because of education, experience, and knowledge of their clients' financial affairs, C.P.A.'s would seem to be the professional most often looked to for financial planning. In recognition of this, the American Institute of C.P.A.'s, in 1987, developed a curriculum of study for those C.P.A.'s desiring to add personal financial planning to their practice.

Before you engage someone as your financial planner, you should inquire as to their educational qualifications and experience. You should also find out if their fee is based on the actual number of hours they will spend working on your plan or from commissions earned on investment products they recommend to you.

There is nothing wrong with accepting commissions. Indeed, such a practice can reduce the direct out-of-pocket cost of a financial plan to you, the consumer. But at the same time, it leads you to wonder if the planner places his pecuniary interests ahead of yours. With a fee based on hours worked, this taint is removed.

In order to put yourself at ease with regard to the fees quoted and the product to be received, discuss the arrangement with your trusted friends and advisors before you commit to anything.

II. *Chapter 10 Math Computations*

A financial calculator is necessary to perform most of these calculations.

A. *Inflation Adjustment*-page 123

What is the future value of $1.00 invested at 4% for 27 years?

Future value equals present value multiplied by annual inflation rate times the power of years to retirement, or:

$$FV = \$1.00 PV \times (1+.04)^n = \$2.883$$

This calculation shows the value in 27 years (where n equals years to retirement) of $1.00 invested at a 4% annual return. The 4% is the annual assumed inflation rate. It is the increase required to maintain the equivalent purchasing power of the base year. It follows then that $36,000 invested today at 4% per year will grow to $103,788 in 27 years or, simply, $36,000 X 2.883. (The 2.883 does double duty as a factor as well as a dollar amount where $1.00 is used as present value. This convention is also used below in section C.)

B. *Retirement Accumulation*-page 123

In the example used, after tax earnings will be 7% annually but inflation will be 4%. In order to calculate the net annual increase, divide 1.07 by 1.04 and state as a percentage increase, or:

$$1.07 \div 1.04 = 1.0288462 - 1.00 = .0288462 \times 100$$
$$= 2.88462\%$$

William's estimated life expectancy at age 65 is 15 years. What accumulation at that time will allow him to withdraw $103,788 (adjusted annually for inflation) per year for 15 years? For calculation purposes, this is an annuity problem where the annual withdrawal represents an annuity payment to William.

Present value equals years of retirement multiplied by percentage increase in the fund reduced by annual payments from the fund, or

PVAD=15 yrs. X 2.88462 X withdrawals of $103,788
$$= \$1,285,459$$

PVAD represents the present value of the fund at the end of William's 65th year. The withdrawals are considered to start at the beginning of each year. Table B-1 illustrates these calculations.

C. *Deflation Adjustment*-page 124

This calculation is the opposite of A. above. What is the present value of a future dollar when inflation averages 4% per year? The present value equals the future value divided by the annual inflation rate times the power of years to retirement, or:

$$PV=\$1.00FV + (1+.04)^n=\$0.3468$$

The deflator multiplied by the accumulation needed at retirement (where n equals 27 years) will yield the present value of the fund today, or $1,285,459 X .3468 equals the present value of $445,797.

D. *Annual Savings Required-Year 1*-page 124

Now that we know the present value of the dollars we need to accumulate, we can calculate the present value of the first year's savings. Knowing this, we can then compute the 2nd through 27th year by applying the annual inflation rate.

In today's dollars, the accumulation needed in 27 years as calculated above is $445,797. Using this sum as the required future accumulation, we calculate the first year savings.

If $1.00 were invested each year for 27 years at an interest rate of 2.8846%, the fund would grow to $40.0425. Since the future sum required in our example is $445,797, it follows that $445,797 divided by $40.0425 will give us the annual savings required the first year or $11,133. Adjusted for 4% annual inflation, the deposit made at the **end** of the first year will be $ 11,578.

Table B-2 illustrates the annual savings, adjusted for inflation, William needs to set aside in his retirement fund each year.

E. *Mary-Principal Sum Needed*-page 124

Mary needs to accumulate $1,095,562 at retirement to provide her with an annual income of $76,689 which is equal to $35,000 in today's dollars.

$$FV = 20 \text{ yrs. } X \ 4\% \ X \ \$1.00 = \$2.191$$

The future value factor of 2.191 multiplied by $35,000 equals a retirement income in 20 years of $76,689.

Since Mary needs an annual income of $76,689 at retirement and can earn 7% after tax (10% before tax but we are only interested in what she is left with to live on), she needs to accumulate a fund of $1,095,562. This is computed by dividing $76,689 by 7%, or:

$$\$76,689 + .07 = \$1,095,562$$

Mary doesn't want to diminish her beginning principal but if she doesn't add to it during retirement, she will lose purchasing power because she is drawing out all of the earnings annually. Clearly, Mary needs to reevaluate her estimated needs during retirement.

Proper financial planning is not static. Needs, and therefore goals, change. Once the initial plan is implemented, it should be constantly monitored to insure that it is fulfilling one's current objectives.

TABLE B-1   William's Withdrawals during Years of Retirement

Year	Withdraw Beginning of Year	Balance after Withdraw	7% Earnings on Balance Left	Balance at end of Year
0				1,285,459
1	103,788	1,181,671	82,717	1,264,388
2	107,940	1,156,448	80,951	1,237,400
3	112,257	1,125,143	78,760	1,203,903
4	116,747	1,087,155	76,101	1,163,256
5	121,417	1,041,839	72,929	1,114,768
6	126,274	988,494	69,195	1,057,688
7	131,325	926,363	64,845	991,209
8	136,578	854,631	59,824	914,455
9	142,041	772,414	54,069	826,483
10	147,723	678,760	47,513	726,273
11	153,632	572,642	40,085	612,727
12	159,777	452,950	31,706	484,656
13	166,168	318,488	22,294	340,783
14	172,815	167,968	11,758	179,726
15	179,726	0	0	0

TABLE B-2   William's Planned Retirement Accumulation

Year	7% Earnings on Prior Balance	Inflation Adjusted Deposit Required at End of Year	Balance in Fund at End of Year
0			0
1	0	11,578	11,578
2	810	12,041	24,430
3	1,710	12,523	38,662
4	2,706	13,024	54,392
5	3,807	13,545	71,745
6	5,022	14,086	90,853
7	6,360	14,650	111,863
8	7,830	15,236	134,929
9	9,445	15,845	160,219
10	11,215	16,479	187,914
11	13,154	17,138	218,206
12	15,274	17,824	251,304
13	17,591	18,537	287,432
14	20,120	19,278	326,831
15	22,878	20,049	369,758
16	25,883	20,851	416,493
17	29,154	21,685	467,332

Year	7% Earnings on Prior Balance	Inflation Adjusted Deposit Required at End of Year	Balance in Fund at End of Year
18	32,713	22,553	522,598
19	36,582	23,455	582,635
20	40,784	24,393	647,813
21	45,347	25,369	718,528
22	50,297	26,384	795,209
23	55,665	27,439	878,313
24	61,482	28,536	968,331
25	67,783	29,678	1,065,792
26	74,605	30,865	1,171,263
27	81,988	32,100	*1,285,459

*Adjusted for rounding difference of $108.

Glossary

attorney-in-fact: the party in a power of attorney who is given the right to act for the person giving the power of attorney, who is called the *principal*.

cohabitation: legally, to live as husband and wife.

common law: the body of law that originated in England, (1) in contrast to the civil law of Rome; (2) in contrast to the equity of the chancery courts of England; and (3) as distinguished from ecclesiastical laws of the church. Today, in Anglo-American jurisdictions, common law is distinguished from laws which are created by statute. When used as a noun, the term does not have a hyphen; when used as an adjective, it is hyphenated.

common-law, or informal, marriage: generally, a marriage which is created by an agreement to marry, followed by cohabitation and a public recognition of the relationship as a marriage, in contrast to a ceremonial marriage.

community property: property owned by a husband and wife in common, with each owning an undivided one-half interest by reason of their marital status.

concubinage: the cohabitation of parties not legally married.

concubine: a woman who lives in a state of unmarried cohabitation.

consortium: the conjugal fellowship of husband and wife, including the right to the company, cooperation and aid of the other. The term is used in tort actions as a right which carries compensatory damages to one spouse for the injury or death of the other.

contract: a promise, or set of promises, either oral or written, either implied or express.

equity: that which is just and fair; a system of law that corrects failures of justice.

filius nullius: an illegitimate child, literally, the child of no one.

inter-vivos trust: literally, "between living persons," the term is used to distinguish between a trust created in a will and a trust created during a person's lifetime.

irrevocable trust: a trust which cannot be revoked.

joint tenants: tenants who have one and the same interest in land, arising from one and the same conveyance, beginning at the same time, and held in the same, undivided possession.

last will and testament: The term arises from the division in ecclesiastical court and common law courts in medieval times. "Will" is an Anglo-Saxon word and "testament" comes from Latin. The two terms arose because the church had jurisdiction over personal property and the state over real property. Today, common usage of the term is used to describe an instrument which seeks to devise all property after death.

meretricious: an unlawful sexual connection.

notorious cohabitation: the statutory offense committed by two parties who live together openly although not married to one another.

palimony: the court-ordered allowance paid by one cohabitant to another.

putative spouse: a reputed spouse unaware of a legal impediment to a marriage.

principal: the party who gives the power of attorney to another party, called the *attorney-in-fact.*

quantum meruit: the reasonable value of services.

resulting trust: a trust which arises by implication of law when it appears from the nature of the transaction between the parties that there was an intention to create a trust.

revocable trust: a trust which can be revoked.

separate property: property owned by a married person in his or her own right during marriage. In a community property state, separate property would be defined as property acquired before marriage or after marriage by inheritance or gift.

tenants in common: tenants who hold the same land, but whose interests may arise under different titles and in distinct shares.

testamentary trust: a trust created in a last will and testament to take effect after death, in contrast to an inter-vivos trust.

trust: literally, the confidence placed in a person in whom legal ownership of property is placed to hold or use for the benefit of another person.

wrongful death: laws which provide recovery for damages after the death of a person by his heirs, enacted by every state to override the common rule that the death of an individual did not give rise to a cause of action in a civil suit.

void marriages: a marriage with no legal force or effect.

Index

ABOUT THE AUTHORS

Johnette Duff and George Truitt share a house, have a cat (hers), a dog (theirs), a hot tub and a trash compactor. He refuses to mow the lawn, and she still hasn't learned how to fold his socks. She's an attorney who handles family law cases in her private practice, and he's a tax partner for a Houston accounting firm, as well as a certified financial planner.

SUNNY BEACH PUBLICATIONS
2180 North Loop West, Suite 120
Houston, Texas 77018
(713) 686-7300
1-800-621-1358

1. Do you have any questions which have not been answered by this book?

2. Are there any areas of the subject matter you would like to see covered in more detail?

3. Have you had any experiences as a spousal equivalent which you would like to share with others?

Please write to us at our offices above and let us have your input. We would like to incorporate your questions and comments in the next edition of *The Spousal Equivalent Handbook.*

Order Form

Please send me _____ copies of *The Spousal Equivalent Handbook* at $12.95 per copy, plus $2 shipping. Texas residents please include applicable sales tax. Or call our toll-free number and order by phone. Visa and Mastercard accepted.

Name_____

Address_____

City_____State_____Zip_____

Visa/MC Account#:_____Expiration Date:_____

THE SPOUSAL EQUIVALENT CENTER
2180 North Loop West, Suite 120
Houston, Texas 77018
(713) 686-7300
1-800-621-1358

In order to keep our readers up to date between editions of this book, we will begin publishing *The Spousal Equivalent Newsletter* on October 1, 1991. This quarterly newsletter will keep spousal equivalents everywhere current on the laws and any other events which impact on their lives.

Along with the legal and financial updates, we will also have a column for spousal equivalents to write in and ask questions, as well as comment on their experiences. This sharing of information, along with such frivolous items as a line of special occasion cards for spousal equivalents (tired of only finding "Happy Anniversary to My Husband" and "Happy Valentine's Day to My Wife" cards?), will make this newsletter both informative and fun.

An annual subscription to the newsletter is $15.00 per year.

===

Order Form

Please sign me up for a year's subscription to *The Spousal Equivalent Newsletter* at $15. Visa and Mastercard accepted.

Name_____

Address_____

City_____State_____Zip_____

Visa/MC Account#:_____Expiration Date:____

===